OLYMPIC
MOMENTS

Published by Times Books
An imprint of HarperCollins Publishers
Westerhill Road, Bishopbriggs, Glasgow G64 2QT
www.harpercollins.co.uk

HarperCollins Publishers
Macken House, 39/40 Mayor Street Upper
Dublin 1, D01 C9W8, Ireland

First edition 2024

The contents of this publication are believed correct at the time of printing.
Nevertheless the publisher can accept no responsibility for errors or omissions,
changes in the detail given or for any expense or loss thereby caused.

The Publishers acknowledge that views around language and sensitivity in journalism are continually changing.
However the language, style and format of the articles in this book have been preserved from
when they originally appeared in the newspaper and should be read in that context.

A catalogue record for this book is available from the British Library

Thanks and acknowledgements go to Robin Ashton and Joanne Lovey at News Licensing and, in
particular, at The Times, Ian Brunskill and, at HarperCollins, Samuel Fitzgerald, Harley Griffiths,
Kevin Robbins and Rachel Weaver. With special thanks to News UK Archives.

ISBN 978-0-00-866425-1

10 9 8 7 6 5 4 3 2 1

Printed in India

If you would like to comment on any aspect of this book,
please contact us at the above address or online.
e-mail: times.books@harpercollins.co.uk

www.timesbooks.co.uk

This book contains FSC™ certified paper and other controlled
sources to ensure responsible forest management.

For more information visit: www.harpercollins.co.uk/green

THE TIMES

OLYMPIC
MOMENTS

John Goodbody and Robert Dineen

Contents

Foreword

By Sir Steve Redgrave

The Olympics have been such a major part of my life, ever since I was 10 years old. In 1972, I used to collect the milk and newspapers delivered to the family home. I remember reading the headlines about the swimmer Mark Spitz and how he won seven golds. As a kid interested in sport, I thought it would be fantastic to win a medal.

The year 1976 was my first rowing and, although there was not much coverage of the sport, I did think to myself, "Why not try to get to the Olympics in rowing?"

That almost happened in 1980, when the quadruple sculls crew, of which I was a member, was the only British men's boat not to go to Moscow. I was extremely bitter, and it still rankles. Would I have won a medal? Who knows? Those Moscow Games were boycotted by several countries, such as the United States, because of the Soviet Union's invasion of Afghanistan. I do not think sport should be used as a substitute for real diplomacy or political pressure. If you are going to place sanctions on a country, then there should be a boycott on everything. Sport should not be singled out. In 1980, the Americans were selling grain to the Soviet Union, but their athletes could not go to the Games.

I had been to three world championships before the 1984 Games in Los Angeles, where I won my first Olympic gold. Richard Burnell, a rower who himself had won Olympic gold for Britain, said to me: "You are a world champion for one year; you are an Olympic champion for life." That summed it up. I became a member of an exclusive club with people like Seb Coe and Daley Thompson.

The Olympics really resonate with people. And as rowing takes place in its first week, if you have been successful, the second week is so exciting as you are able to enjoy watching other sports. You recognise that you are just one part of the ultimate event.

In 1988, Andy Holmes and I were in the coxless and coxed pairs, so had to race every day. We won the coxless pairs and, unlike 1984 when everything happened so quickly, I really enjoyed the celebrations with family and friends. But the next day, we had the final of the coxed pairs and the fact that we had already won one gold affected our attitude. We finished third.

Four years later, by then with Matt Pinsent, I had to compete having been diagnosed with ulcerative colitis, for which I still take medication. Despite this initial setback, we had what turned out to be our three best races together – the heats, semi-final and final. We won by almost five seconds.

Matt and I were together for three Olympics.

I needed as much from him as he did from me. We fed off each other's strengths. Winning my fourth gold in 1996 led to a breakthrough with the media and in public consciousness. At the time I think I coped well with the pressure. I must admit that I didn't remember saying what I did to the BBC immediately after the win in Atlanta: that if anyone saw me near a rowing boat again, they had permission to shoot me. At the time, I had expected that it was going to be my last race, but those words were said with raw emotion at a particular time.

My decision to continue until 2000 was complicated by suffering from diabetes, which I managed then and still do now. One reason for continuing was that when someone else won, I would be watching, thinking that I should have been there. In Sydney, I knew in the last 500 metres that we were going to win. Still the pain at the end was probably the worst I have ever experienced. Clearly, aged 38, it was the right time to retire, with five gold medals.

One of the first things that happened after those Games was that I was let into the secret that London was going to bid for the 2012 Olympics. While there is an emptiness after retiring, the fact that I was immediately involved in that meant the dream went on. There was a huge satisfaction in continuing to have a role in the Olympic Movement.

My broadcasting work with the BBC started at the 2004 Games. My punditry role involved providing an insight into what the competitors would be feeling before events. It also gave me the freedom to go to other sports. My involvement in the Olympics has continued in other ways, too, such as being an ambassador for Team GB and coaching the Chinese rowing team.

Over the years, the Olympics have had to adapt and evolve. One big change came in 1984 when the Los Angeles Games was the first one to make a profit. Cities want to bid for them now as bidding alone provides benefits.

Though Manchester was twice unsuccessful in trying to get the Games, it meant that the city got a velodrome, which has been the centre for Britain's successful cycling teams.

Every Games has had problems. There have been boycotts, hold-ups in construction, and controversies. But I still feel that the Olympics are needed. They benefit society and the athletes themselves long after the event itself is over, and provide thrilling entertainment along the way.

Introduction

By John Goodbody and Robert Dineen

The Summer Olympic Games are not just the largest and most widely watched sports event in the world, they provide a unique platform for competitions that consistently provide more dramatic and emotional stories than any other. In creating the modern Games in 1896, the Frenchman Baron de Coubertin took inspiration from the fabled events staged in Greece from 776 BC until Emperor Theodosius I abolished them in 393 AD. These ancient competitions were known to be rich in myth and drama, and their modern counterpart has lived up to that reputation. Ever since Coubertin's revival of the model, the Olympics have offered a colourful kaleidoscope of memorable performances, scandals, and personal and collective sadness.

The publicity of the Olympics turns many individuals into global stars. Muhammad Ali, then known as Cassius Clay, first attracted attention when winning a gold medal in 1960. The first perfect score of ten in Olympic gymnastics by the Romanian Nadia Comaneci made her an international celebrity. The same happened to Mark Spitz, with his seven gold medals in one Games, and to Michael Phelps, an even more successful American swimmer. Usain Bolt's sprint victories, beginning in 2008, earned him an exalted place in sporting folklore, as did five successive gold medals for the British oarsman Sir Steve Redgrave.

However, what makes the Games so compulsive is that beneath the giants of sport, there are thousands of competitors trying to achieve their own personal best performances, having devoted years of training to become an Olympian and being determined to carry that status with honour. As Simon Barnes, the former chief sportswriter of *The Times*, wrote: "Everywhere you go at the Olympics, you meet someone having the most important day of their lives."

What makes the Olympics so widespread in global interest is that sports that are popular in certain countries are little known in others. To give one example, volleyball is not a major sport in Britain. Yet, the biggest international television viewing figure at the 2008 Games (excluding the opening and closing ceremonies) was not for Usain Bolt's 100 or 200 metres triumphs but came when China played a volleyball match. More than 250 million people watched that event, almost all of them Chinese.

Over the years, *The Times* has also covered the news stories that have occurred before, during and after the Games. The tension is so high at the Olympics, it is almost inevitable that there are incidents that supersede the sports themselves. There was the sight of the Black American athlete Jesse Owens taking four athletics gold medals in 1936 before a German crowd conditioned by Hitler's pronouncement of the superiority of the Aryan race. Just after troops from the Soviet Union had invaded Hungary in 1956, there was a brutal water polo match between the two countries. And there was the famous 'Black Power' demonstration by American sprinters in 1968. All these – and many others – are dwarfed in significance by the killing of members of the Israeli team by Palestinian terrorists at the 1972 Olympics in Munich. That was the darkest hour in the history of the Games.

All these events have been covered by journalists for *The Times* and their work is collected in this book. Unlike the men's football World Cup, in which no British team participated for the first 20 years, individuals from this country did take part in the first staging of the Games. At those Olympics in Athens, they won eight medals, although *The Times* did not send a reporter. There was more extensive coverage in the newspaper in 1908, when London hosted the Games for the first time and it dutifully recorded the collapse and subsequent disqualification of Dorando Pietri in the marathon, an incident which started the fascination with the longest running race in the Games.

Our search of the archives threw up some surprises. As you will read, two of the most lauded British moments in the history of the Olympics, Harold Abrahams's victory in the 100 metres and that of Eric Liddell in the 400 metres, were reported with gentlemanly restraint by 'A Special Correspondent' in the newspaper in 1924. It was only when the Oscar-winning film Chariots of Fire was first screened in 1981 that their performances and their backgrounds, admittedly somewhat embellished, achieved national recognition.

Although *The Times* steadily increased its coverage of sport after the Second World War by sending more specialist reporters, often some of the most interesting stories of the Games, especially those involving foreign competitors, were not reported. In these cases, we have leaned heavily on *The Sunday Times*, for which John wrote a weekly series of the 100 Greatest Moments of the Games in the build-up to London 2012.

These original omissions are even more true for the Paralympics. We have selected outstanding competitors from those Games, which now follow the Olympics in the same host city. Only really with the 2012 Games did the Paralympics come to prominence in Britain but they have maintained a constant presence in the media in subsequent years. The problem with reporting on the Paralympics is that, because it requires you to compare different categories and different events, it is difficult to assess the value of performances. However, we have tried to choose those individuals who have been recognised as particularly outstanding in the international community. These have included such Britons as Dame Sarah Storey, Dame Tanni Grey-Thompson and Ellie Simmonds. Their contribution, both as competitors and as figureheads, has transformed the public's perception both of disability sport and, more importantly, of disability itself.

The Paralympics have certainly been of immense value socially across the world but so have the Olympics, where, for example, the increasing number of women's events has compelled men particularly to change their views about the role of female athletes. The victory of Britain's women's hockey team in 2016 was also a blow against homophobia since two leading members, Helen and Kate Richardson-Walsh, were married.

This is why the Olympics, despite all the scandals, political difficulties and controversies, remain such a noble event. Their global interest bestows increased prominence on important social issues, while providing so many athletes with purpose, and so many people with the thrill of watching the events live and then reading about them in *The Times*.

LEGENDS

Didrikson triumphed on track and field

Women's high jump | Athletics

Los Angeles, 1932

No other sportswoman showed such versatile talent at the Los Angeles Olympics as Mildred "Babe" Didrikson, who added silver medal in the high jump to the gold that the United States athlete won in both the 80 metres hurdles and the javelin. Didrikson cleared the same height in the high jump as her compatriot Jean Shiley, only for officials to separate them on the grounds that Didrikson's 'head-first' style was improper.

That winning leap of 5ft 5½in was a world record. Didrikson, who won five events at the US trials but was restricted to entering three by the Olympic rules, also set a world record in the 80 metres hurdles of 11⁴⁄₅s. She was awarded gold ahead of compatriot Evelyne Hall, albeit the two women were given the same time. Didrikson won the javelin with an Olympic record of 47 yards 2¼ft.

One of six children of Norwegian migrants, Didrikson was born in Texas and as a youngster excelled at physical activities. After reading about the 1928 Olympics, she decided to focus on the 1932 Games. She even persuaded neighbours to cut their hedges so she could practise hurdling over them.

For Los Angeles, Didrikson had to choose three events and was upset with the decision not to award her gold in the high jump, pointing out that she had used the same style throughout the competition without any issue.

By John Goodbody

Mildred "Babe" Didrikson (far right) leads the field on her way to winning the 80 metres hurdles at the 1932 Games in Los Angeles.

Owens strikes a blow against Hitler

Men's sprint relay | Athletics

Berlin, 1936

Jesse Owens not only completed his domination of the 1936 Olympics in Berlin, but he provided the perfect riposte to Adolf Hitler, the leader of Nazi Germany.

The Black American athlete, having triumphed in the 100 metres, 200 metres and long jump, helped his country's sprint relay team to win gold in front of Hitler, who had intended to use the Games for international propaganda.

The US team set a world record of 39⁴⁄₅s in the final, leaving Italy to take silver and Nazi Germany bronze. It was Owens's second world record of the Games, having set another to win the 200 metres ahead of Mack Robinson, another Black American who took silver. He beat a third Black team-mate Ralph Metcalfe, to win the 100 metres. As impressive as each of those achievements were, it was the events in the long jump which were to become Olympic folklore.

Owens, believing he was warming up in qualifying, took one easy leap, only to find that it was judged one of his three official attempts. He fouled his second. Luz Long, his German rival, then approached the American and suggested that to make certain he progressed, he should jump from well behind the board. Owens did so but qualified by only 1cm.

The final was titanic. Owens began by setting an Olympic record of 7.75m and then improved to 7.87m. Long reached the same distance. Owens then responded, first reaching 8.01m and then, with his last jump, 8.06m. Long was the first to congratulate him, chatting in the full gaze of Hitler.

The grandson of an enslaved man, Owens was one of 11 children and by the age of seven was picking cotton in the Alabama fields. When the family moved north to Cleveland he was enrolled at a local school and when asked to identify himself gave the initials of his first names, James Cleveland, saying "JC".

The teacher misunderstood and wrote "Jesse". Having won the US trials, Owens went to Berlin as one of what the Nazi newspaper Der Angriff (The Attack) termed the "Black auxiliaries" of the American team.

By John Goodbody

Top Left – Jesse Owens, of the United States, breaks the tape to win the 100 metres at the 1936 Berlin Games, which were attended by Adolf Hitler.

Bottom Left – Owens on the podium after winning the long jump. Luz Long, the German silver medallist, salutes Adolf Hitler in the crowd. Naoto Tajima of Japan claimed bronze.

Flying Dutchwoman completes hat-trick

Women's 200 metres | Athletics

London, 1948

FROM OUR SPECIAL CORRESPONDENT

Mrs Fanny Blankers-Koen, of Holland, confirmed her status as the greatest all-round woman athlete yet seen at an Olympic Games with victory in the final of the women's 200 metres.

The Dutchwoman raced home about 2½ yards in front of Miss Audrey Williamson, of Great Britain, to claim her third title in London. She has already triumphed in the 100 metres and the 80 metres hurdles.

For once, Mrs Blankers-Koen did not break a record – there was, of course, no Olympic record to break, for this was the first time that the event had been included in the programme.

She was drawn in the inside, with Miss Shirley Strickland, of Australia, outside her and Miss Williamson in the middle of the field of six. Mrs Blankers-Koen quickly gained on the forward runners and, after entering the straight, was perhaps five yards in front of Miss Strickland.

About 10 yards farther on, Miss Williamson forged a little ahead of the others but could not make up the ground to Mrs Blankers-Koen, who won by less than a couple of her rapidly shortening strides. Weakening visibly after a prolonged all-out effort on the sodden track, she was white and looked strained at the finish, but her time of 24.4s was a fine one in the conditions.

Fanny Blankers-Koen, of Holland, breaks the tape to win gold at London 1948.

Zátopek's feat of endurance

Men's marathon | Athletics

Helsinki, 1952

FROM OUR OLYMPIC GAMES CORRESPONDENT

The athletics in the Olympic stadium had very nearly ended this evening with the arrival of the marathon runners, headed by no less a person than Emil Zátopek who, true to his promise, not only entered his first race over the 26 miles 385 yards but won it apparently without any concession to doubt or distance.

No one could grudge this amazing personality from Czechoslovakia his latest triumph. It was an unprecedented feat to win a 5,000 metres, a 10,000 metres and a marathon in the course of a week or so. Zátopek's time of 2hr 23min 3.2s was an Olympic record.

The appearance of Zátopek among the 60 runners who lined up in four rows for the start of a marathon which, even before it began, looked full of dynamite, added to the tenseness of the atmosphere.

The route was two and a half laps around the stadium and then the main highway leading from Helsinki to the North, with a turn round approximately 13 miles and back over the same route to the stadium, where about three-quarters of a lap remained to be run.

The road surface was supposed to be good enough, but the ups and downs were rather more severe than the Windsor to Chiswick course at the Polytechnic Marathon in and around London a few weeks ago. The day was cloudy and cool.

One really ought to have felt alarmed when, at 20 kilometres, Zátopek raced into a lead. One could almost see him doing it. Running behind anyone has never been to his liking and a little thing like a marathon was clearly not going to alter his mood and method. Britain's Jim Peters, the winner in London, was now 10 seconds behind the leader but, with Gustaf Janssen, of Sweden, keeping up what obviously was a stiff pace. Reinaldo Gorno, the Argentine, and his compatriot Delfo Cabrera were there.

At the 30th kilometre, Peters had fallen a minute behind Zátopek. Even that, however, did not prepare one for the shock when, at 35 kilometres, the name of Peters dropped entirely out of the announcements. Thenceforward the interest lay in whether Zátopek could maintain the pace he had set after the first 12 miles, but all doubt vanished when he entered the stadium apparently not nearly as tired as when he won the 5,000 metres.

Instead Zátopek reached the tape actually smiling for a change, as well he might.

Opposite Top – Emil Zátopek (right) on his way to winning the marathon at Helsinki 1952.

Opposite Bottom – Zátopek leads the 5,000 metres field at Helsinki 1952, en route to winning the second of his three golds for Czechoslovakia at the Games.

Cassius Clay shows substance beneath swagger

Men's light-heavyweight | Boxing

Rome, 1960

From a *Times* reporter

Cassius Clay defeated Zbigniew Pietrzykowski, of Poland, to win the light-heavyweight title at the Olympic Games. The American demonstrated skill to win all five rounds on the judges' scorecard and earn victory by a margin of 5-0.

Pietrzykowski, the bronze medallist at the Games four years ago, is eight years older than the 18-year-old Clay, but was no match for the fighter from Louisville, Kentucky.

Clay has been a star in the Olympic Village, revelling in the atmosphere, chatting exuberantly with fellow athletes and having his picture taken with everybody who fancied the experience, including the American singer Bing Crosby. As the British journalist George Whiting, who witnessed Ali's talent for the first time in Rome, pointed out: "You might fault six-footer Clay for flashiness but there was no doubting his ability when the need arose."

In the press conference after his final, Clay was questioned by a Soviet Union journalist, who pointed out that, as a Black man, he could not eat in some United States restaurants because of the 'Colour Bar'.

Although Clay knew this, he launched a fierce defence of his homeland, saying: "I got lots of places I can eat – more places I can than I can't."

Cassius Clay throws a punch against Soviet boxer Gennady Schatkov at the 1960 Olympics.

Fraser finds glory after tragic year

Women's 100 metres freestyle | Swimming

Tokyo, 1964

From Our Swimming Correspondent

After what she described as the most desperate finish of her life, Miss Dawn Fraser, of Australia, tonight became the first woman to win three successive Olympic 100 metres freestyle titles.

Miss Fraser did not exaggerate. It was only in the last third of the final length of a thrilling struggle with Miss Sharon Stouder, of the United States, that the brawny Australian girl, at the ripe old swimming age of 27, broke away and fulfilled all the hopes that lay so heavily upon her.

Thirteen years of training were behind this third victory for Miss Fraser and nearly a year of sadness after the car accident in which her mother was killed and she, herself, injured.

The reigning champion made a good start, but when she turned, in 27.8s, Miss Stouder, aged just 15, was only just behind.

In the next 15 to 20 yards the battle was won and lost. First there seemed little in it and the Australians sitting next to me sucked in their breath in dismay. One whispered, unbelievably, "Dawnie's had it". It seemed almost blasphemous, and it took a supreme effort by Miss Fraser in the next half-length to crawl.

Miss Fraser admitted afterwards that in the moment the thought was in her mind that she would not win. "I could see Sharon was there and I felt pretty tense."

Dawn Fraser, of Australia, looks relaxed ahead of winning gold in the 100 metres freestyle at Tokyo 1964.

Super-human Spitz takes seventh gold

Men's 4 x 100 metres medley relay | Swimming

Munich, 1972

FROM NORMAN FOX

Nobody in history has so dominated an Olympic Games like Mark Spitz. On the eighth and last day of the swimming competition here, the American won his seventh gold medal. In his every final Spitz has broken the world record.

The seventh victory came as part of a team but was nonetheless significant. He swam the butterfly leg of the 4 x 100 metres medley relay so superbly that he ensured the gold medal for the United States after East Germany had threatened to take a firm hold on the race.

Spitz took over with nothing between the two teams. By the end of his 100 metres, he was able to hand over a lead for the final leg of about two metres. The hard individualist had played his part for the team and so they won in 3min 48.16s, easily beating the old record. East Germany just held off Canada for the silver.

Spitz had earlier taken his sixth gold by winning the 100 metres freestyle in 51.22s. He had spoken in his guarded, clinical way of being tired and of having back pains. Two defeats, in the heats and semi-final round by Michael Wenden, of Australia, pointed to the chance of an upset. But Spitz had been kidding us. In the final he led almost from the start; not by more than a hand or two at first, but the gap increased as he thrashed the water and his rivals.

Mark Spitz races to victory in the 100 metres butterfly at Munich 1972, the fourth of his seven golds at the Games.

Comăneci captures hearts with perfect performance

Women's individual all-around | Gymnastics

Montreal, 1976

FROM JIM RAILTON

Nadia Comăneci, Romania's 14-year-old European champion, became the new superstar of women's gymnastics today by winning the combined-individual exercises with a series of perfect marks of 10 in the asymmetrical bars and the beam. Her cool and professional presentation captured the crowd once more and led to a standing ovation.

The silver medal went to the Soviet Union's popular Nelli Kim and the bronze to her team-mate Ludmilla Tourischeva, the former Olympic overall champion, who generously embraced both of her young conquerors before receiving her own medal.

While Olga Korbut, although not the perfect gymnast in Munich, entranced a worldwide audience with her charm and gaiety, the mechanical precision of Comăneci took over here in every sense this afternoon.

The competition was pure theatre. Each of the favourites showed her form on the tricky beam, the treacherous asymmetrical bars, the canvas ballroom of the floor exercises and in flight at the vault. Each was announced by electronic flashers from cameras like moths gathering for their fate around an overheated bulb. Next came the sighs, applause and so often boos as the subjective judges did not meet the approval of a subjective audience.

At least twice the judges and spectators were at one. Comăneci received the greatest applause when being given her medal after a spectacular exhibition which was nearly but not quite equalled in decibels as Turishcheva accepted the minor award in such a sporting spirit.

Nadia Comăneci performs a back handspring during her beam routine at the 1976 Olympics.

Zorn bows out as greatest ever

Women's S12 100 metres backstroke | Swimming

Athens Paralympics, 2004

The extraordinary career of Trischa Zorn was over. It ended with an event that brought her yet another medal to increase her standing as the most successful Paralympian competitor in history, with a total of 41 gold medals, eight silver and five bronze.

As the 40-year-old blind American secured a bronze in the 100 metres backstroke in the S12 category, her fellow competitors, officials and spectators joined in the applause for someone who had given so much to the Paralympic Movement. She had wanted to take part in these Games after her fortieth birthday because the Games had meant so much to her and because it was a tribute to her mother, who died from breast cancer in June of that year. Zorn carried the flag at the closing ceremony, which her mother had always attended in the past.

Zorn had taken part in every edition of these Games since 1980 and for many of her fellow countrymen she became a symbol of the event. Blind from birth, she developed into a remarkable all-around swimmer. After growing up in Orange County, California, Zorn became a four-time American backstroker whilst at the University of Nebraska, where she was the first visually-impaired athlete to be awarded a Division One Scholarship in the National Collegiate Athletic Association.

By John Goodbody

America's blind swimmer Trischa Zorn at the 2000 Paralympics in Sydney, where she won four silver medals. She bowed out four years later with a total of 54 medals.

Lewis takes giant leap to greatness

Men's long jump | Athletics

Atlanta, 1996

FROM DAVID POWELL, ATHLETICS CORRESPONDENT

The sands of time were kind to Carl Lewis. They did not run out before he could complete the story of an Olympic legend. The sand he took away with him, in a polythene bag from the pit of the Centennial Stadium here, was his personal souvenir of the night that, at 35, he won a fourth consecutive long jump gold medal.

He joined Al Oerter, discus champion from 1956 to 1972, as co-holder of a record four victories in the same event. He might have been looking at an outright record tenth gold in the sprint relay, but the United States have not selected him.

Roger Black said that not choosing Michael Johnson for the 4 x 400 metres in the 1991 world championships was "the biggest mistake that the American selectors have ever made", but they have just surpassed it. Who in the world would not have wanted to see Lewis storming to victory, as he surely would have, on the last leg of the relay?

At no stage this season had Lewis looked the likely winner, not until he produced his victorious third-round jump of 8.50 metres. The path that had led him to that moment had been scarred with potholes.

Having failed to qualify for the US team for the 100 and 200 metres at the trials, Lewis was perilously close to elimination from the long jump, too. He squeezed into the team, taking the third and last place, by three centimetres.

Again he was facing elimination when, in the qualifying round on Sunday, he was in fifteenth place with one chance to come. The pressure on, he jumped into first place. No wonder he said, as he walked into a packed press conference having won the final: "I want to know how you all got into my dream. I do not think I woke up this morning."

Then Lewis continued with a summary of his work ethic. "I think I have given a professional perspective," he said. "You have to present yourself well, you have to look good, you have to speak well."

At his first Olympics, in Los Angeles in 1984, Lewis was jeered when he passed on his last jump. He did not take it here, either. He said he forgot in all the commotion of his victory having "been sealed".

"When I wake up tomorrow, I want to look at my clock and make sure it is the next day and that I did not wake up just this morning," he said.

Carl Lewis, aged 35, seizes long jump gold for the United States with his third effort in the final at Atlanta 1996.

Redgrave gold makes it five in a row

Men's coxless fours | Rowing

Sydney, 2000

From John Goodbody and David Watts

Steve Redgrave entered the history books last night when he won an astonishing fifth gold medal in five consecutive Olympics. The victory in the coxless fours final sets him up to become the first rower to be knighted for his achievements in the sport.

The Olympic title capped the most remarkable career in the history of British Olympic sport with a stunning performance on the first overcast day of the Olympics. After the race Redgrave turned to his crewmates and said: "Remember these six minutes for the rest of your lives. Listen to the crowd and take it all in. This is the stuff of dreams."

He triumphed before a full house of 22,000 while millions more watched at home and around the world as he and his team-mates Matthew Pinsent, who has now won three Olympic gold medals in succession, James Cracknell and Tim Foster won by a margin of 0.38 seconds over the Italian silver medallists.

Redgrave's eldest daughter, Natalie, nine, was in floods of tears as the boats crossed the line: the finish was so close that she thought her father had failed to make it. Her sisters were also overcome by the moment. Even afterwards, all Natalie could say was: "It's good."

Shortly before the gold medals were presented by the Princess Royal, a drained and emotional Redgrave said: "After 250 metres had gone, I thought we had won. It was all over in my eyes. As soon as we are in front, no one comes past us. Second place is not good enough with these guys."

Matthew Pinsent hugs Steve Redgrave after the British crew, won gold in the coxless fours at Sydney 2000. Tim Foster (far left) and James Cracknell (far right) slump forwards.

When told of the split-second margin of the victory, Redgrave said: "It was enough. It doesn't really matter, does it? We just had to focus on the job." Pinsent paid tribute to his colleague. He said: "Winning a fifth gold makes Steve the greatest Olympian Britain and arguably the world has ever produced. He is an inspiration to all of us in the boat and the whole rowing world."

Along the banks Union Flags far outnumbered those of other countries, leaving even the host nation in the shade. Britain's greatest oarsman now looks likely to retire. He has twice threatened to do so before in Seoul after the 1988 Olympics and again after the Atlanta Games four years ago. His glittering career includes nine world championships and three Commonwealth championships.

The British four took the title over the tree-lined 2,000 metres course in 5min 56.24s. They set a stupendous pace leading from the start and quickly establishing a half-length lead. The Italians, who had beaten the British crew in Lucerne in July, began their move after 1,000 metres and over the last 250 metres attacked repeatedly.

The British crew, cheered on by thousands of their countrymen, held on in the cacophony of noise. Pinsent punched the air and clambered over Foster to embrace Redgrave, whose ability to row himself to exhaustion is celebrated. Redgrave just collapsed over his oars, hardly able to smile at his unprecedented triumph.

The British crew of (left to right) James Cracknell, Steve Redgrave, Tim Foster and Matthew Pinsent salute the crowd after winning gold.

Grey-Thompson anointed greatest Briton

Women's T53 400 metres | Paralympic athletics

Athens, 2004

FROM MATTHEW PRYOR

Tanni Grey-Thompson carved her name in the record books by powering away from the rest of the field in the T53 women's 400 metres to win her eleventh Paralympic gold and become Britain's most successful Paralympian in the modern era.

The gold, her second of these Games after the 100 metres, took her past the ten golds won by Caz Walton, the former Great Britain fencer.

"It [the medal record] means more to me than my world records because it might last longer," an ebullient Grey-Thompson said. "I was so nervous this morning I really struggled to warm up. I was feeling all right for about ten minutes when I woke up then I had my first trip to the bathroom to be sick." At least she was not sick on the side of the track before the starter's gun, as she had been before winning the 400 metres at Sydney 2000.

"It's a good day to die," Ian Thompson, Grey-Thompson's husband and coach, told her as she wheeled on to the track. That is exactly what Grey-Thompson did. "I had nothing left in the last two metres, I was dying," she said.

The 400 metres was Grey-Thompson's strongest event of the Games and although her time of 57.36s was more than a second outside her world record of 56.28s, set last August, she still won by almost a second.

Tanni Grey-Thompson competes in the T53 wheelchair 100 metres at Athens 2004, to which she went on to add victory in the 400 metres.

Jim Thorpe at the 1912 Olympics, where the
Native American won the decathlon and
pentathlon for the United States.

At last, justice for Thorpe

Men's pentathlon and decathlon | Athletics

Stockholm, 1912

BY A *TIMES* REPORTER (1983)

Replicas of the two gold medals confiscated from Jim Thorpe, the American athlete, after the 1912 Olympic Games in Stockholm, were given to his family yesterday – after 70 years.

Thorpe overcame a deprived upbringing to lead a remarkable sporting career. Of American Indian origin through his parents, both of whom died by the time he was 15, he had a native name, Bright Path.

At the Stockholm Games he began by winning the pentathlon in athletics and then triumphed in the decathlon. However, in 1913, a newspaper disclosed that before the Games Thorpe had played professional baseball. The rules on amateurism were strict.

Thorpe wrote to the Amateur Athletic Union, the governing body in the United States, saying: "I hope I will be partly excused by the fact that I was an Indian schoolboy and did not know about such things." The letter was sent to no avail.

Thorpe joined the New York Giants baseball team and excelled in American football, as the highest-paid player for the Canton Bulldogs.

His later life was marred by poverty and alcoholism. After his death in 1953 campaigners called for his medals to be reinstated. Among those opposing the move was fellow American Avery Brundage, the IOC president from 1952-72, who had finished sixth in the pentathlon in 1912.

In 1973 the American Athletic Union decided his baseball earnings could be considered legitimate expenses and restored his amateur status.

Thorpe in training.

Phelps wins most coveted gold

Men's 200 metres butterfly | Swimming

Rio de Janeiro, 2016

From Craig Lord

Michael Phelps's status as the greatest Olympian in history was safely secured before he arrived in Rio de Janeiro. However, after reclaiming his 200 metres butterfly title in the early hours of yesterday – a night when he took his tally of gold medals to 21 – the American said that he could finally declare his comeback a success.

Phelps quit the pool after London 2012, where he won four more golds but lost the 200 metres butterfly crown to Chad le Clos. In 2014, the American decided that he could not let that defeat go.

The 200 metres butterfly has always been special to Phelps – it was the event in which he became an Olympian in 2000 aged 15 and in which he set his first world record at 16 – and provided the motivation for his return. He has won back his title, though, finishing in 1min 53.36s, with Le Clos fourth.

"Just to be able to see the No. 1 next to my name again in the 200 butterfly, it couldn't have been scripted any better," Phelps said. "That being my very first Olympic event, to be able to win it at my fifth Olympics, it's pretty special. I told Bob [Bowman, his coach] when I came back how bad I wanted that 200 'fly. I came in on a mission."

The victory also earned Phelps his 12th individual gold, equalling the all-time Olympic record set by Leonidas of Rhodes – in 152 BC.

Michael Phelps on his way to retaining his title in the final of the 200 metres butterfly at the 2016 Games in Rio de Janeiro. It was his 21st gold.

Farah seals historic 'double double'

Men's 5,000 metres | Athletics

Rio de Janeiro, 2016

FROM JAMES HIDER

Mo Farah wrote his way into the history books by winning gold in the 5,000 metres, adding it to his triumph in the 10,000 metres and thereby becoming the first Olympian since Lasse Viren in 1976 to defend successfully the two middle-distance titles.

Farah, having repeated his triumphs of London 2012, said: "It shows I didn't just fluke it in London. To do it again is incredible. I can't believe it." Farah dedicated his gold medals to his children. "This medal is for my son. When I'm gone, all my kids will have something of me," he said.

His success capped Britain's most successful Olympics in more than a century and ensured a place higher in the table than China and higher than Team GB at London 2012.

As the Games drew to a close, all eyes had been focused on Farah, whose campaign had almost come undone a week earlier when he was tripped up by his training partner during the 10,000 metres. He had

also tripped in the 5,000 metres heats and complained that he was still stiff from last week's epic run in the 10,000 metres final.

There were no upsets last night and Farah started out at a comfortable pace at the back of the field before picking off his competitors one by one in the last five laps. In the final push, he stormed past Paul Chelimo, of the United States, and Hagos Gebrhiwet, of Ethiopia, who won silver and bronze.

Farah said: "Mentally I had to be on top of my game – the guys were out there to get me – so I just had to be alert. You saw me sat at the back, but it wasn't an easy last five lap burnout. The guys pushed on and on.

"At the beginning I felt a bit tired, but I got going again. I went to the front and I know the guys were thinking about me, so I controlled the race. I wasn't going to let anyone past me. Then just at the end I used my speed."

Mo Farah wins the 5,000 metres at Rio 2016, adding to his victory in the 10,000 metres at the same Games. He was the first man since Lasse Viren to retain the two Olympic titles.

Bolt silences sceptics with display for ages

Men's 100 metres | Athletics

Rio de Janeiro, 2016

FROM MATT DICKINSON, CHIEF SPORTS WRITER

The most delicious anticipation falls over a stadium in the momentary, pin-drop silence just before the 100 metres. The air crackles with infinite possibilities. But last night only one question hung heavily in the Brazil night sky – was Usain Bolt still The Man, still the king of Planet Sport? The answer came, triumphantly, in 9.81s.

The strutting, swaggering reign of Usain continues. He has no equal, not now, not ever. The greatest of today, the greatest of all time. Think of a superlative and double it. Athletics needs all the uplifting narratives it can get in desperate times and Bolt has made the world smile along with him once more. He did not need victory to prove anything but he did it anyway, a third successive Olympic victory in the 100 metres distinguishing him – even more than ever – from any human being who ever lived.

The 100 metres has always been a race of villains and superheroes – for every Jesse Owens, a Ben Johnson – and, in many eyes, this race boiled down to seeing whether Bolt could still maintain his hold over a man convicted of two doping offences. If he had lost, especially to Gatlin, to many it would have felt like seeing Superman fall under a train or discovering at the end of Finding Nemo that the cute fish ends up deep-fried and eaten with chips.

Bolt had nothing to prove but the world was still desperate that he did. Sport likes upsets but it also worships excellence, and this was one event where everyone swung behind the favourite although he arrived with more questions to answer than usual. His double double of the 100 metres and 200 metres in Beijing and London was already unique in history (buffed up by two more golds in the 4 x 100 metres relays).

Yet, arriving in Brazil, he had not been leaving the world trailing in his wake quite so easily. His world-record times – of 9.58s in the 100 metres and 19.19s in the 200 metres, both in Berlin at the World Championships – are seven years old, and feel like it. When he ran 9.79s to win the world title in Beijing last year, defeat was perilously close. Gatlin, the fastest man in the world, might have had him but for dipping for the line too early, losing by one hundredth of a second.

In a sceptical world, this slowing process could be said to be reassuring. Bolt has at least shown a little mortality approaching his 30th birthday, which falls on Sunday; the day of the closing ceremony. It will be party night in the Olympic village and Bolt has something very special to celebrate.

Usain Bolt celebrates winning the 100 metres at the Rio de Janeiro Games in 2016. The victory silenced sceptics who said Bolt's powers were waning.

Bolt crosses the line to win
the 100 metres.

GREAT TEAMS

Magical Magyars upset old order

Men's football

Helsinki, 1952

The great Hungarian football team of the 1950s first attracted fame by winning the 1952 Olympic title, though they are known more for being the first country from outside the British Isles to beat England at Wembley, winning 6-3 in 1953 and, a year later, crushing England 7-1 in Budapest.

Spectators at the 1952 Games saw several outstanding Hungarians, such as goalkeeper Gyula Grosics, nicknamed The Black Panther, József Bozsik, a supplier of penetrating passes, and the two strikers Sándor Kocsis and Ferenc Puskás.

Hungary overwhelmed all their rivals in Finland, scoring a total of 20 goals and conceding two. The victory over England in 1953 has often been seen as the moment the home of football realised its failings. Internationally, it was a turning point, with more than 100 foreign journalists witnessing the defeat of the old masters by a team renowned throughout the continent, having by then gone 33 matches without defeat.

Because of the smog cloaking London, they had to return by Tube rather than coach to their hotel. Grosics told me on a later visit to London: "When we got out at Baker Street the fog was so thick we had to walk back to our hotel holding hands so we could not get lost. We sang Hungarian folk songs through the streets to celebrate our victory." The team were welcomed home by 200,000 people in Budapest.

By John Goodbody

England keep out a Hungarian attempt on goal during the match between the two sides at Wembley in 1953. Hungary went on to win 6-3, the first country from outside the British Isles to beat England at Wembley.

Factory workers conquer world

Women's volleyball

Tokyo, 1964

Perhaps no team have had to confront such massive expectations as the Japanese women's volleyball squad when the sport made its debut at the Tokyo Olympics.

In the late 1950s, a team was formed at the Nichibo company's spinning mill in Kaizuka, near Osaka. They came under the direction of their martinet coach, Hirofumi Daimatsu. After work finished at 3.30pm, the group would start up to six hours' training. He would hit them and shout at them. Masae Kasai, the captain, said: "I often wished the ball would hit him in the face."

The team won all four big domestic tournaments, then turned their attention to the international arena. They dethroned the Soviet Union in Moscow at the 1962 world championships. They also introduced techniques that are commonplace now, but were revolutionary then.

The Olympic tournament in Tokyo nearly did not take place when North Korea withdrew, reducing the countries to five, one too few to be sanctioned. So, Japan paid South Korea a million yen to enter the event, where they failed to win a set.

Nothing was going to stop Japan revelling in their expected triumph. The Japanese team lost only one set on their charge to the final. It was watched by a television audience beaten only once before in the nation's history. The Soviet Union fought hard and saved four match points before Japan won.

Cue hysteria in the Komazawa venue and relief across the country.

By John Goodbody

Masae Kasai, captain of the Japanese volleyball team, leaps for a hit in the gold-medal match against the Soviet Union at the 1964 Games.

Hungary put rivals to sword

Men's team sabre | Fencing

Rome, 1960

Hungary's supremacy in the sabre lasted from 1908-64. Their fencers won every individual title, except for 1920, when Hungary were barred because of their role in the First World War. They also took seven successive Olympic team titles.

Aladár Gerevich was their star, winning gold medals at every Olympics from 1932-60, the last when he was 50. Hungarians have long been renowned for their swordsmanship, a necessary quality given their many struggles against Turkish invaders. In 1908, the first time London hosted the Games, five of the top six represented Hungary. This domination led to the number of entrants from one country being limited to three. Four years later Gerevich took a bronze medal in the individual competition, won by a compatriot, Endre Kabos.

Hungary captured the team title. Among that team was the 24-year-old Pál Kovács, two years younger than Gerevich and called 'Foxy' for his cunning. Gerevich won the Olympic title in London in 1948 and the silver medal four years later in Helsinki, with Kovács taking gold. The pair enjoyed team success at those Games, although Gerevich had initially been told he was too old. Those 1960 Games were the last for Gerevich and Kovács.

Richard Cohen, who represented Britain in the sabre at three Olympics and is the author of *By The Sword*, the definitive history of the sport, says: "Gerevich was technically outstanding and possessed wonderful footwork."

By John Goodbody

Hungary's talisman fencer Aladár Gerevich in action against Italy's Gastone Dare at London 1948. Gerevich won gold at every Olympics from 1932 to 1960.

British success signals new era

Men's hockey

Seoul, 1988

From Sydney Friskin

Great Britain, who had begun their Olympic challenge on a note of uncertainty, finished it with awesome efficiency on Saturday as they achieved an emphatic 3-1 victory over West Germany in the final.

With the Netherlands winning bronze, Olympic hockey returned to its original European stronghold. At Antwerp 68 years ago, all three medals were presented to European countries, England (representing Great Britain), Denmark and Belgium. India and Pakistan, the two great powers from the Asian sub-continent, gold medal winners in 1980 and 1984 respectively, were out of the top four places for the first time since 1928.

From the transition to artificial surfaces has emerged a new breed of hockey player, his athletic strength blending with a fair amount of skill and his mind attuned to European tactics based on firm defence and bustling forward play.

Britain, ably guided by Roger Self, the manager, and David Whitaker, a tactical genius, knew exactly what to expect from the Germans after being beaten 2-1 by them in the group match. What the British team achieved, however, on Saturday drew high praise all round, the consensus being that if you beat Australia and West Germany you must be the best team in the world.

It has also been generally accepted that in Sean Kerly, Steve Batchelor and Imran Sherwani, Britain have the three best forwards in the world, all having played prominent parts in Saturday's victory. Behind them were eight defenders whose main purpose was to manoeuvre the ball to midfield and let the forwards do the rest.

The first crack in the German defence was discovered by Sherwani, who accepted Kerly's pass and went on to put Britain ahead in the twentieth minute.

Britain's more variable drill at short corners brought unexpected riches in the eleventh minute of the second half, a subtle flick by Paul Barber to his left enabling Kerly to scoop the ball high into the net for his eighth goal of the tournament.

A chip shot worked wonders for Britain when Barber lofted the ball from deep in his own area to Batchelor, lurking near the 23-yard line. A square pass to Sherwani caused a great roar in the stands as he drove the ball into goal. Heiner Dopp scored for the Germans with about 10 minutes remaining but they had nothing more after that.

Britain's male hockey players celebrate during their triumphant campaign at the 1988 Games.

Dream Team divide sport

Men's basketball

Barcelona, 1992

FROM A *TIMES* REPORTER

Dream Team it may be, but it is unlikely to be a recurring one. So, the rest of the basketball world can now sleep easier. The United States men's side duly won the surest gold of these Games in Barcelona on Saturday, 117-85 over Croatia, and then the criticism of team selection started, from within, no less.

The US Olympic team chief, LeRoy Walker, said the unprecedented decision to pick National Basketball Association (NBA) professionals had left no room for Olympic hopefuls from American college basketball and pledged it would not happen for the 1996 Games.

"I don't want every youngster who has a dream of making the Olympic team to feel that he can't do this unless he makes the NBA," Walker, who is favoured to become the next president of the US Olympic Committee, said.

The American team was invited to play in the Olympics by a selection committee of the professional NBA and the USA Basketball Federation. Quite simply, it was the greatest team ever to be assembled. Michael Jordan, Earvin "Magic" Johnson, Charles Barkley, Larry Bird and David Robinson were just the icing on the cake. Eleven of the 12 players are legitimate superstars in the NBA. They are all millionaires, to boot.

Walker said he wanted Olympic basketball players selected by try-out. "I don't believe that there aren't some college players who could fit into this process and we could still have our best team."

Germany's Michael Jackel (left) tries to get past Patrick Ewing, of the United States, as team-mate Karl Malone holds off Hans Gnad at the 1992 Games. The United States's "Dream Team" was their first Olympic squad to field active NBA players.

British crew smash pain barrier

Men's coxless fours | Rowing

Athens, 2004

FROM ANDREW LONGMORE, FOR *THE SUNDAY TIMES*

Steve Williams was pondering the meaning of suffering. "You put your body in a place where you ask it a question and it's a simple answer. Yes or no," said the bowman of the victorious British tour. Multiply the suffering by eight, four on each side, and the pain of yesterday's finale of the coxless fours cannot be measured on the scale of ordinary mortals. At the climax of an epic duel with the Canadian crew, the coxless four of Matthew Pinsent, Ed Coode, James Cracknell and Williams crammed so much hope, despair, emotion, time and sheer physical distress into their final, decisive 10 strokes, you feared their boat might sink under the weight.

Behind Pinsent, in the seat occupied by Partridge for much of the season, sat Coode, a fringe member of the British squad until Alex Partridge suffered a collapsed lung seven weeks ago. "I don't know what the 'over the moon' feeling is," said Coode yesterday. "But my feet certainly aren't on the ground. I kept going for another four years to get this medal round my neck."

So many circles neatly turned, so many lives fulfilled or fractured by the eight hundredths of a second that separated the defending Olympic champions from the world champions at the finish. The result was so close the officials had to call for a photo.

After a year of pain and torment, Great Britain's men's coxless four won the gold medal in Athens by four inches. Neither crew dared to believe they had

Matthew Pinsent, Ed Coode, James Cracknell and Steve Williams celebrate victory in the men's coxless fours. It meant Pinsent had won gold in four successive Games.

won. "We didn't know," said Barney Williams, stroke of the Canadian four. "Then the flags started waving and we realised they weren't Canadian flags."

In the British boat, Cracknell's shout crossed four years' worth of pain barriers, while Pinsent slumped backwards: he had just won gold in a fourth successive Games. Coode screamed and Williams, ever taciturn, barely raised a smile. "Sometimes I think this is exactly what I was meant to do," said Williams later, "but there have been so many days that have been colossal days, that you think, 'yes, definitely, this is great' in the morning and in the afternoon say 'no way, I'm not doing this again'." But now? "Now this is an all right feeling."

The final promised a duel between two top-class crews. "With about 40 strokes to go, Steve Williams made a call for a push, but I couldn't really hear it because of the noise." said Pinsent. "I thought. 'Okay. let's just nail it for 30 strokes'. I counted off 30 in my head and looked around and we still seemed to be down. I couldn't believe it. With ten left, there was no alternative but to finish it off. I really didn't think we'd won but two things were in our favour. One was the surge of the boat seemed right: two, they didn't believe they'd won either." A classic drama fit for a classical setting.

Team GB's (left to right) Steve Williams, James Cracknell, Ed Coode and Matthew Pinsent during their heat at the Athens Olympics.

Britain light up Rio with hockey heroics

Women's hockey

Rio de Janeiro, 2016

By Julia Gregory

Great Britain's women's hockey team have won their first Olympic gold, beating the Netherlands in a penalty shootout.

The final finished 3-3 in normal time after the British keeper, Maddie Hinch, 27, nicknamed "Mad Dog", pulled off a series of remarkable saves. The Dutch could not get past her in the shootout either, which ended 2-0 after Helen Richardson-Walsh and Hollie Webb scored penalties to claim Britain's twenty-fourth gold medal of the Olympics.

"It's difficult to put into words what this means," said Richardson-Walsh. "Seventeen years ago, when I started my career, we were so far off this. It has taken so much hard work and it means absolutely everything."

Helen Richardson-Walsh, and her partner, Kate, who is the captain, became the first married couple to win gold for Britain since Cyril and Dorothy Wright in the sailing in 1920. Helen said: "To get an Olympic medal is special but to share it with Kate is truly amazing." Kate, 36, added: "To see Helen go through double-back surgery and maybe never play again – she took that penalty and it was so assured."

She confirmed, however, that it would be her final appearance for Great Britain. "One hundred per cent I will retire as a reigning European champion with England and an Olympic champion."

Britain, coached for 11 years by Danny Kerry, began the Games having slipped to seventh in the world rankings after a disappointing Champions Trophy in London in June. In Rio they became the only team to progress from the group stage unbeaten, overcoming Argentina and Australia, ranked second and third in the world respectively, and then defeating Spain in the quarter-finals.

Kerry said: "We know we're good at shootouts. As soon as it went there I knew we would win. Eight of the group are multiple Olympians and we needed that experience today."

Hinch described the victory as a "huge team effort", adding, "Goalkeeping has its highs and lows. You can be a villain, but you can also be a hero. It helped that the Dutch had a shootout in their semi-final, so that gave me a chance to see what they do."

Nicola White, the Great Britain forward whose last-quarter strike levelled the match at 3-3, said: "This is what we dreamed of and now we've got it. No one can ever take that away from us. We always knew it was going to be very close but physically we stuck to it. We really put the legwork in to try and get them on the counter and get up the pitch."

The British women's hockey team celebrate on the pitch during their gold medal-winning campaign in 2016.

DUELS

Nurmi doubles up in remarkable feat

Men's 1,500 metres and 5,000 metres | Athletics

Paris, 1924

From Our Special Correspondent

The stadium at Colombes was again today strewn with bits of broken records, thanks to the efforts of the remarkable Paavo Nurmi. The Finn did the mile (1,500 metres) in 3min 53⅗s, which is 3⅙s better than the Olympic record, which has stood since 1912.

An hour after this performance Nurmi did three miles (5,000 metres) in 14min 31⅕s, which beats the Olympic record by 5⅖s. Ville Ritola – these Finns appear to be invincible – who finished two yards behind Nurmi, without anyone else within 200 yards, must also have beaten the Olympic record by some five seconds and, had Ritola really pushed him, Nurmi could undoubtedly have done better.

As if to underline his extraordinary ability in Paris, he had checked his watch and dropped it on the in-field with just more than a lap left. He did not need mechanical assistance to understand that he was on track to make history.

Paavo Nurmi, of Finland, wins the 5,000 metres at the 1924 Olympic Games.

Stephens crowned new queen of speed

Women's 100 metres | Athletics

Berlin, 1936

FROM OUR SPECIAL CORRESPONDENT

She is aged just 18 but Miss Helen Stephens, of the United States, appears invincible in the sprint events on the track. Pitted against Miss Walasiewicz of Poland – better known as Stella Walsh – in the final of the 100 metres, Miss Stephens led from the front against the previous queen of speed and held on to win by more than two-tenths of a second.

Miss Walsh, the Polish champion, actually ran faster than she had ever done, finishing in 11.7 seconds. Miss Stephens's time of 11.5s was not quite so fast as her world record of 11.4s on the previous day. But on a wet and windy day, it was still ample enough to win in front of Herr Hitler, who has been a regular attendant at the Games, and is no more fortunate than the ordinary spectator – the whole stadium is in the open.

Helen Stephens, of the United States, wins the 100 metres from Poland's Stella Walasiewicz at Berlin 1936.

Irresistible Kuts
breaks British hearts

Men's 5,000 metres | Athletics

Melbourne, 1956

FROM OUR OLYMPIC GAMES CORRESPONDENT

Britons are used to disappointments in Olympic athletics, perhaps because we often expect too much, forgetting how strong the opposition is from other nations. But this afternoon at the cricket ground here there came the biggest blow so far when Vladimir Kuts of Russia won the 5,000 metres and crushed one of Britain's finest athletes in Gordon Pirie, winning by 80 metres an event in which it seemed so certain to many that we would have the victor.

All else on a warm busy afternoon in the stadium paled by comparison with this race and few of the Olympic champions acclaimed so far can have made as deep an impression as Kuts. The Russian won with a formidable display of front running that few thought was sensible in this event.

He took the lead halfway through the opening lap, rolling slightly, storming his way up to the front as if to say "here comes the medicine, see if you can take it".

Medicine it was, for the stocky Kuts took the field round the first 400 metres in 63.5s. Two more laps of 66 apiece and the British pair of Pirie and Derek Ibbotson were beginning to make their presence felt. The fourth lap was a second slower at 67s. But Kuts had put in the first of his bursts, more delicate than in the 10,000 metres, as if taking the pulse of his rivals. Sixty-six, 66, 66 went the fourth, fifth, and sixth laps and now it was the Russian scarlet followed by two white British vests.

The tenth lap took only 69s, but here the battle was won and lost, at least as far as the public were concerned. As Kuts went steadily ahead, by five, 10, 15 yards, Pirie and Ibbotson were broken.

As Kuts broke the tape 80 yards to the good, all eyes turned to Pirie and Ibbotson, who were now fighting it out for second place. Ibbotson went once on the back straight, but Pirie went with him and, with 20 yards to go, Pirie put in such a searing finish that Ibbotson's head went back in anguish and he almost walked in.

Opposite Top - *Vladimir Kuts, of the Soviet Union, leads from Great Britain's Gordon Pirie in the epic 10,000 metres final of 1956.*

Opposite Bottom - *Kuts leads from the British trio of (right to left) Gordon Pirie, Derek Ibbotson and Chris Chataway in the 5,000 metres final of 1956.*

Johnson hangs on for nail-biting victory

Men's decathlon | Athletics

Rome, 1960

FROM OUR ATHLETICS CORRESPONDENT

At 9.25pm tonight, Rafer Johnson retained the Olympic decathlon title for the United States with perhaps the most dramatic finish that has ever been seen in this event.

In the last event of the 10 that comprise this gruelling test, the 1,500 metres, he was drawn in the same heat as his only rival, Yang Chuan-kwang, of Taiwan. Hurried calculations revealed that Johnson, the world record holder, had only to finish about 6.5s behind Yang to win after finishing the ninth event, the javelin, 65 points in front.

All eyes were on Yang and Johnson as they wearily lapped the track, Johnson determinedly sticking to Yang's shadow after two days of exhausting competition. Yang tried to force the pace, his face contorted with the effort. Yet Johnson, ruthlessly driving his 6ft 3in, 14st 4lb along, stayed just behind.

On the last back straight Yang struck desperately. He opened a gap of three yards as he latched on to another athlete who was going past, but suddenly found he could not keep up the change in pace and Johnson regained contact round the last bend.

In the home straight Yang was rolling with fatigue and so was Johnson, but still they kept together until the last 25 yards, when Yang at last opened a gap. It was not nearly enough and Johnson, with a new Olympic record of 8,392 points, had won the title by just 58 points.

Rafer Johnson, of the United States, completes the 100 metres during his triumphant decathlon campaign at Rome 1960.

Heaviest athlete crashes to earth

Men's +100kg | Greco-Roman wrestling

Munich, 1972

When the American Chris Taylor marched on to the mat for the first round of the Greco-Roman wrestling, he was the heaviest man to compete in the Games in any sport in the 20th century. He weighed 182kg (more than 30 stone) and combined his bulk with acute tactical sense.

Opposing him was Wilfried Dietrich, a German, nicknamed "the Crane of Schifferstadt", his hometown, because of his ability to lever opponents skywards. Dietrich had won more Olympic medals than anyone else in wrestling history, a gold, two silvers and two bronzes, and aged 38 was competing in his fifth Games but weighed only 118 kg.

Richard Barraclough, a British wrestler in Munich, said: "No one expected that anyone would throw Taylor." But after only 14 seconds, Dietrich clasped his hands round Taylor's ample chest, locking arms as was necessary in this style of wrestling, then used the forward momentum of the American to throw him in a movement known as a salto. He continued the action, rolling Taylor on to his back and pinning his shoulders on to the mat to secure an outright victory.

The German crowd were first stunned, then ecstatic. Dietrich was so euphoric that he lost his focus for the rest of the competition and was disqualified in the third round. He retired after Munich, but is always remembered for perhaps the most famous throw in the sport.

By John Goodbody

Wilfried Dietrich, of West Germany, claims one of wrestling's most spectacular victories by throwing the American Chris Taylor over his back in the +100kg Greco-Roman event. Dietrich weighed only 118kg compared to Taylor, who at 182kg (more than 30st), was the heaviest man to compete in the Games in any sport in the 20th century.

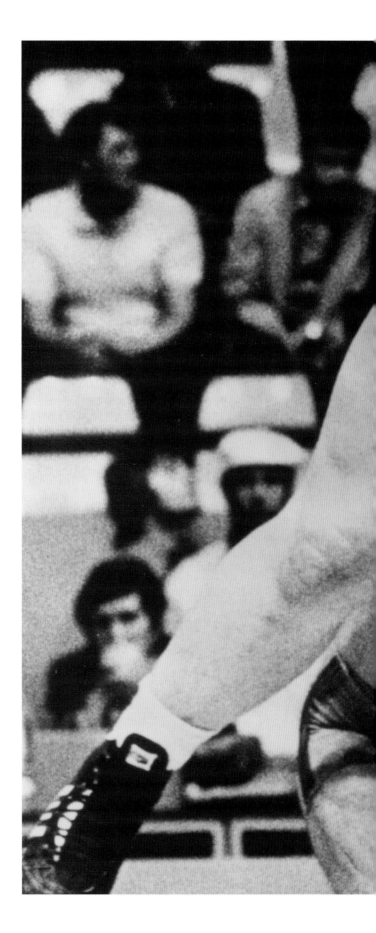

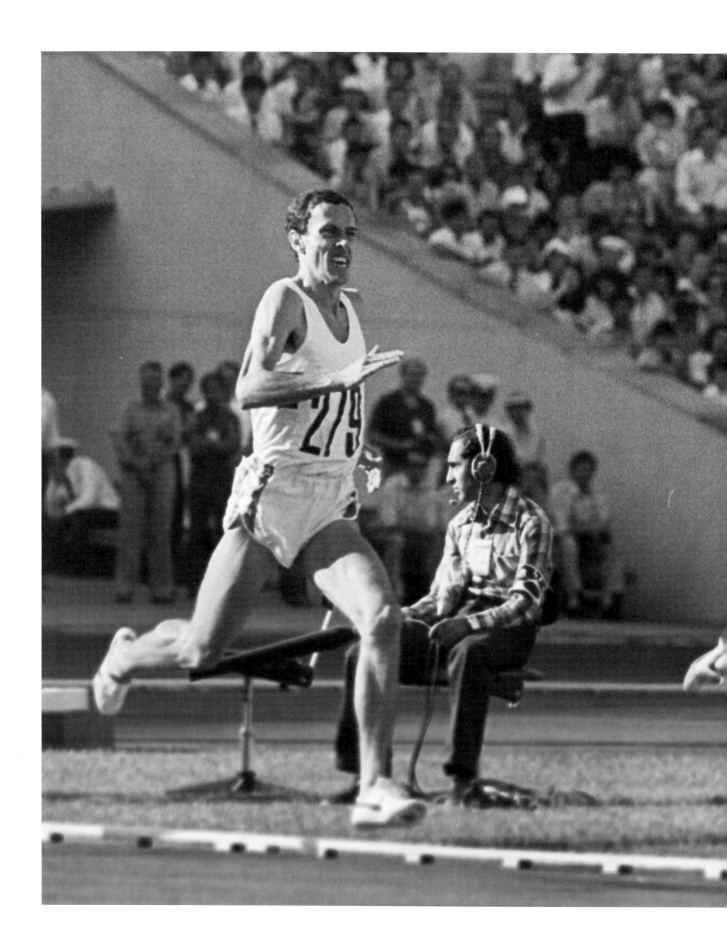

Coe claims shock revenge

Men's 1,500 metres | Athletics

Moscow, 1980

FROM CLIFF TEMPLE, FOR *THE SUNDAY TIMES*

So, it ended one-all: two own goals, some might even say. If the confrontations here in Moscow between Sebastian Coe and Steve Ovett were less than classic races, the very fact that the underdog in each case won is the sort of stuff which keeps the sport alive. Ten days ago any athletics follower, told that the two Britons would win one gold medal apiece, would have awarded the 800 metres to Coe and the 1,500 metres to Ovett, not the other way round. It proved both can still win, but both can lose at their specialities as well.

"Above all," said an unshaven Coe, clutching a cardboard cup of breakfast coffee in the Olympic Village yesterday, "it will have taken a lot of pressure off us both. We may be racing each other quite regularly during the next three or four years, but now that the big confrontation is out of the way, it may never be like that again.

"There has been tremendous pressure on both of us here and Steve and I agreed, when we were waiting together in the doping control room, that the results here are more those of Olympic pressure than anything." That pressure, which had been weighing more heavily on Coe as world record holder in the 800 metres, and perhaps led to the lack of concentration which almost gave the race to Ovett on a plate, had switched to his rival on Friday night.

Ovett had already won the event no one expected him to (least of all him), so how could he, with 45 consecutive victories in the 1,500 metres and mile across all competitions since April 1977, possibly lose now to Coe, who had so little experience at the

Seb Coe races away from his great rival Steve Ovett to win the 1,500 metres at Moscow 1980. The victory avenged Ovett's triumph over his fellow Briton in the 800 metres.

distance? But he did. It may have been partly due to having to run a much faster heat, equivalent to a 3min 54s mile, than he had expected. But next night there he was in the semi-finals waving to the British section of the crowd before even beginning his kick, while the news was that Coe had been afflicted with Moscow tummy that very day.

How could anyone contemplate then that, with the three fancied Soviet runners already eliminated, the supreme racer could fall at the 46th fence? A sustained drive, initiated by the East German Jurgen Straub, was the perfect tool to blunt Ovett's famed finish. Ovett was fractionally slow to respond and then simply could not match the leg speed or the basic hunger of Coe. They say an antelope can outrun a cheetah if its life depends upon it; to the cheetah it is merely another meal he is chasing. On Friday Coe was the antelope, running to redeem himself – in his own eyes as much as anyone else's. The effect on Ovett was so damaging that he eventually ceded second place to Straub.

Ovett beats Coe in the 800 metres at the 1980 Games. Coe got his revenge in the 1,500 metres.

Thompson triumphs after gruelling battle

Men's decathlon | Athletics

Los Angeles, 1984

FROM PAT BUTCHER, ATHLETICS CORRESPONDENT

Daley Thompson reclaimed his Olympic decathlon title after two days of unremitting struggle with his great rival, Jürgen Hingsen, of West Germany. Thompson fell one point short of Hingsen's world record, but that clearly mattered little to the Briton who slowed down towards the end of the 1,500 metres, the final event, to enjoy his victory.

Thompson had been trailing going into the third and last throw of the discus, the seventh of the 10 events. But the 26-year-old pulled out a personal best, his third of the competition, when his last throw landed at 46.56 metres, to give him an additional 100 points on to the better of his two previous flat throws, and he was back into a lead, albeit well reduced, of 32 points. At this stage in the world championships in Helsinki last year, which he also won from Hingsen, Thompson was 141 points ahead, and his eventual winning margin was 105 points.

Thompson had started the day in an ideal position, having achieved a world record total of 4,633 for the first five events, and held a comfortable 114 points lead from Hingsen overnight.

He owed that lead to personal best performances in the 100 metres, the first event, and the long jump. Thompson was an impressive winner of his 100 metres heat in 10.44 seconds. In the long jump, Thompson added 1cm to his and the previous Olympic decathlon best, jumping 8.01m with his final effort.

Thompson's lead was then reduced, when Hingsen beat him in the shot. Hingsen was expected to close the gap further in the high jump, and duly cleared at 2.12m, despite a brief scare when he appeared to injure a knee on landing. Thompson could manage only 2.03m and his lead was cut by half. Some unlikely storm clouds were gathering over the Coliseum when

Thompson and his now close competitors went to their marks in the 400 metres, the last event of the day. But a time of 46.97 seconds, only slightly outside his best, took Thompson further away again to finish the first day on 4,633 points to Hingsen's 4,519.

Hingsen probably saw his best chance of beating Thompson in five meetings disappear when the West German could only vault 4.50m in the eighth event of the 10. He then watched Thompson go on to clear five metres.

Below – Daley Thompson whistles along to his national anthem after winning decathlon gold in 1984, ahead of two West German opponents, Jürgen Hingsen (left), the silver medallist, and third-placed Siegfried Wentz.

Opposite – Thompson throws the javelin as part of the decathlon competition.

The United States' Mary Decker falls after colliding with Zola Budd of Great Britain during the 3,000 metres in Los Angeles.

Budd taunted over cruel collision

Women's 3,000 metres | Athletics

Los Angeles, 1984

FROM CLIFF TEMPLE, FOR *THE SUNDAY TIMES*

It was the saddest climax to a feverishly awaited duel. After 1,650m of the first women's 3,000 metres final, Zola Budd's legs became entangled with Mary Decker's and sent the American tumbling to the ground.

Some of the home spectators in the crowd were so stunned to see Decker felled that their popcorn never made it right up to their mouths. First stunned, then angry, sections of the spectators began booing Zola, who was left with just her British team-mate, Wendy Sly, and Romania's Maricica Puică for company. Over the last lap Puică kicked away from Sly to win, while the Hounslow girl held on for the silver medal.

Budd, the South African-born athlete whose repatriation had generated such interest, faded to seventh. She appeared traumatised by what had happened with the woman billed as her rival for gold.

The saddest incident relating to the collision, however, was still to come. As the runners filed off the track, most offered a hand of condolence to Decker, who had been carried sobbing from the arena with a torn gluteal muscle. The tiny figure of Budd offered her hand too, but Decker declined to take it, snapping, "Don't bother." It was, perhaps, the most acute moment of rejection for the shy 18-year-old South African. As a schoolgirl in Bloemfontein she had pasted a cut-out picture above her bed of her idol: Mary Decker.

Decker lies on the track in agony after the collision.

African duel signals new harmony

Women's 10,000 metres | Athletics

Barcelona, 1992

FROM JOHN GOODBODY

The end of a titanic women's 10,000 metres in the Olympic stadium symbolised the new harmony in African sport. Derartu Tulu, a Black Ethiopian, and Elana Meyer, a White South African, duelled for the last ten laps after Britain's Liz McColgan, the world champion, had set the early pace only to finish fifth.

After Tulu outsprinted Meyer on the final lap, the pair embraced and ran round the track arm in arm, their flags draped around their shoulders. It demonstrated to the world the international acceptance of South Africa's return to the Games after 32 years' absence. In South Africa the symbolism of that lap of honour was not lost on television viewers. The South African tricolour, banned on the track as a symbol of the apartheid regime, was waved vigorously from the terraces, but Meyer, 26, wrapped herself in the Olympic flag for the triumphant tour of the stadium.

Meyer said afterwards: "It was a very special moment. We did it for Africa. The continent needed two really good women runners. It was so necessary to do this for the whole of my country."

Tulu's victory was a significant advance for Black women athletes, who have not historically done well in long distance running. She is the first Black African woman to win a gold medal on the track. She said she had thought that the race would have been harder than it was.

Left – Ethiopia's Derartu Tulu celebrates her gold in the 10,000 metres at Barcelona 1992, alongside silver medallist Elana Meyer, of South Africa, and Lynn Jennings, the bronze medallist from the United States.

Opposite Right – Tulu leads Meyer in the 10,000 metres at Barcelona's Olympic Stadium.

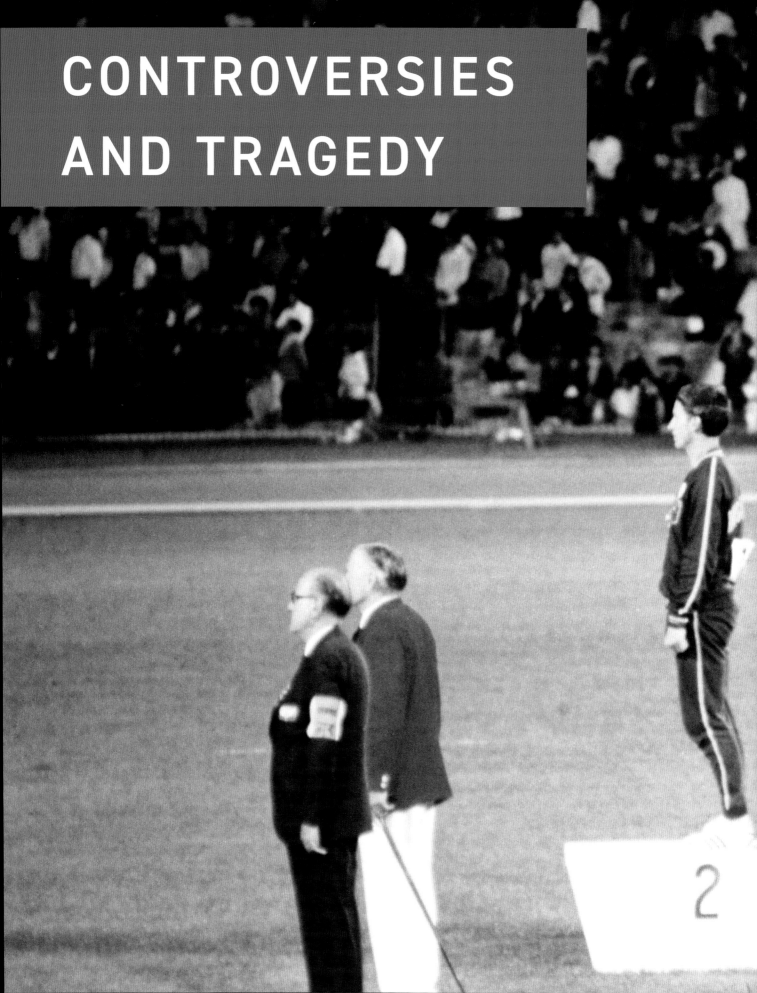

CONTROVERSIES AND TRAGEDY

Irish giant who was denied his hat-trick

Men's hammer | Athletics

Los Angeles, 1932

The hammer thrower Pat O'Callaghan is not only Ireland's greatest Olympic athlete but also lays a formidable claim to be his country's most celebrated sportsman. He won the title in 1928 to bring the Irish Free State its first Olympic gold medal, and repeated the triumph four years later. He would probably have won in 1936 only for sports politics to bar him from competing.

O'Callaghan was wonderfully talented both in sport and in the medical profession, qualifying as a doctor at the age of 20. He learnt to throw the hammer by boring a one-inch hole through a 16lb shot and filling it with the ball-bearing core of a bicycle pedal. His first serious competition was in June 1927, when he reached 136ft 1.5in. Later that summer, he threw 151ft 5.5in to rank him among the top 20 in the world that year. He was not expected to win a medal at the Olympics but, after trailing Ossian Skjöld of Sweden, O'Callaghan borrowed his opponent's hammer and came through to finish first with a throw of 168ft 7in.

On arriving in the United States for the 1932 Games, he was not informed that the event was being held on a cinder surface, rather than grass or clay as was common. His spikes were too long and hampered him on his third turn as he prepared to throw. After qualifying, he borrowed a saw from a groundsman in the Los Angeles Coliseum and cut down his spikes before the final. His second throw of 176ft 11in showed talent rare enough for victory.

The Irish did not send a team to the 1936 Games because the International Amateur Athletic Federation no longer recognised the body that represented the majority of the athletes in the Irish Free State. O'Callaghan remained faithful to the organisation and watched the event from the stands in Berlin.

By John Goodbody

Ireland's Pat O'Callaghan during his triumphant hammer-throw campaign at the 1932 Games in Los Angeles.

Bad blood in the water

Men's water polo

Melbourne, 1956

No summer Olympics have taken place amid such international unrest as the Melbourne Games, which began on November 22, 1956. The political tension burst out in the semi-final of the water polo between Hungary and the Soviet Union, an event later known as 'The Blood in the Water Match'.

Less than four weeks before the Games, Britain, France and Israel had invaded Egypt, nominally to preserve the passage of ships through the Suez Canal. With the Arab nations in uproar, Egypt, Iraq and Lebanon boycotted the Games. Simultaneously the world was focused on an uprising in Hungary against the communist rulers.

By November 1, Soviet Union tanks and troops attacked their satellite state, killing more than 2,000 Hungarians and themselves losing 750 troops. Within days the communists had regained control and many thousands of Hungarians were executed, imprisoned or emigrated. Holland, Switzerland and Spain promptly boycotted the Games.

When the Hungarian Olympic team reached Melbourne, they learnt what had happened and many determined to compete with honour and then defect to the West.

Water polo was one of several sports at which Hungary were supreme in the 1950s. At the semi-final, Hungarians waved their national flag with the Soviet hammer and sickle cut from the middle and chanted "Hajrá Magyarok" ("Go Hungary"). One of the team, Ervin Zádor, said: "We felt we were playing not just for ourselves but for every Hungarian. This game was the only way we could fight back."

The Hungarians taunted the Soviet team, who, in turn, described them as traitors. Player after player from either side was ordered to the sin-bin. When captain Dezső Gyarmati, who was to win five Olympic medals, gave Hungary the lead with a twice-taken penalty, the Soviet team became increasingly frustrated.

Sporadic fighting broke out, with Gyarmati clearly punching one opponent, but Hungary kept on top. They were 4-0 up when Zádor switched positions to mark Valentin Prokopov. Zador took his eye off the Russian to look at the referee. A punch broke his cheek bone and split his face. The referee stopped the game and awarded victory to Hungary. Even without Zádor, Hungary beat Yugoslavia 2-1 in the final.

By John Goodbody

Blood streams from the cut eye of Hungary's Ervin Zádor following a confrontation with a member of the Soviet team in the closing stages of their water polo match at Melbourne 1956.

The crowd shouts and whistles at the Soviet water polo team as the match against Hungary ends in acrimony at Melbourne 1956.

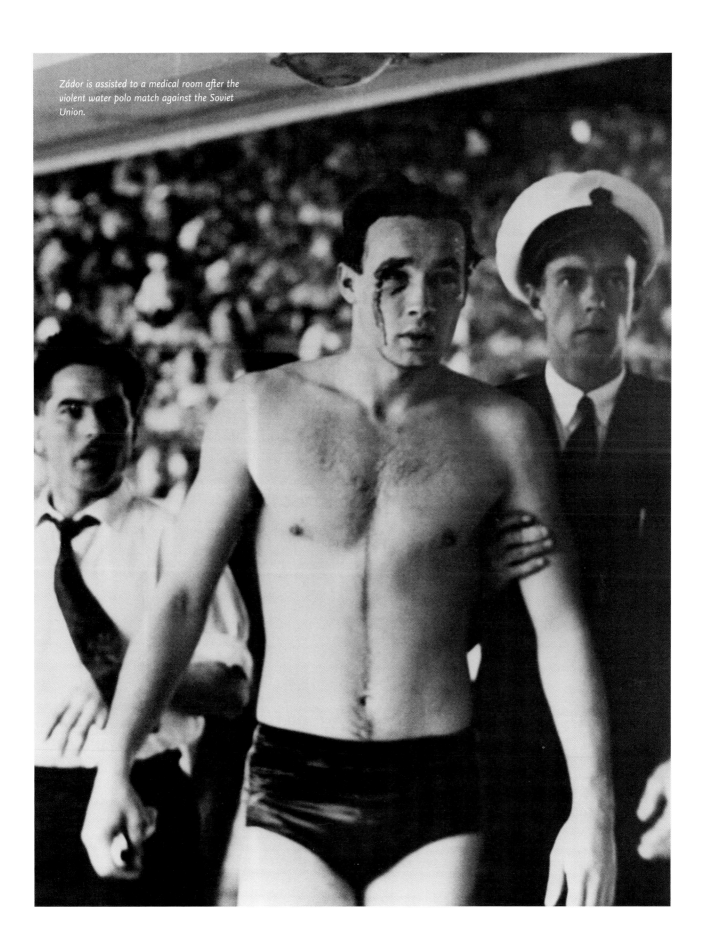

Zádor is assisted to a medical room after the violent water polo match against the Soviet Union.

Brave Americans assert Black power

Men's 200 metres | Athletics

Mexico City, 1968

FROM NEIL ALLEN

No one remembers Olympic winning times for long. Ask any but the most dedicated follower of athletics in a few months hence what was the time of Tommie Smith, of the United States, when he won the 200 metres and there will be some wild guesses. But for as long as the modern Olympics continue the world will remember the scene at the victory ceremony for the 200 metres in the Olympic Stadium here.

Smith, together with the bronze medallist, John Carlos, made sporting history by becoming the first Olympic champions, not to make money, but to make racial political capital out of the most treasured moments of their sporting careers.

I can still see it all, many hours after the watches had stopped and the fanfare had sounded for the medal winners. "It was," as Roger Bannister remarked, "a gesture conducted with dignity and poise and all very memorable."

Smith, the White Australian Peter Norman, and Carlos came out on to the green of the field under the glare of the floodlights. The two Americans walked in black stockinged feet. Their hands were behind their backs, partially shielded by their running shoes but through binoculars we could see that Carlos and Smith each carried one black glove. They wore black scarves round their necks.

The athletes mounted the rostrum and received their medals graciously enough. Then the moment came when they turned to their right towards the flags of the United States and Australia, and The Star Spangled Banner was played. Smith's black-gloved right hand shot out with clenched fist and Carlos, wearing the left glove, made the same gesture. The anthem was played and the two men bowed their heads.

They left the rostrum and marched towards the stand with their arms still stuck out as some of the crowd, mostly Americans, booed and others, chiefly Mexican, cheered. At the press conference afterwards, it was Carlos who reminded the 90 per cent White audience of reporters: "You think of us as animals. Tommie and I heard them boo tonight and we saw their White faces. What I say is, and I want you to print this right or not at all, that White people who go to see Blacks perform and can boo them like they did tonight, should not go to see us at all."

But it was Smith who was the champion and gave the right impetus, by his remarkable victory despite a sore abductor muscle, to this staging of publicity for a national cause. He said: "If I win, I am an American, not a Black American. But if I did something bad, then they would say 'a negro'. We are Black and we are proud of being Black. Black America will understand what we did tonight."

If this great American sprinter, and his friend Carlos, gained any kind of victory by their unprecedented gesture, it may be found in Norman's words as the silver medallist slipped unobtrusively from the interview room.

I asked him why he was wearing the Olympic Project For Human Rights badge, as were the Americans. "Because I asked them for one and because I believe in human rights." "Even in view of the 'keep Australia White' policy?" I asked. "Especially because of the 'keep Australia White' policy," he replied.

Smith had made a lot of enemies but the most notable Black champion of all had gained an ally.

Tommie Smith (centre) and John Carlos (right) perform the Black Power salute during the medal ceremony for the 200 metres at the 1968 Olympics in Mexico City. Australian Peter Norman (left) is wearing a human rights badge in solidarity.

Russian banned over rigged weapon

Men's modern pentathlon

Montreal, 1976

From Neil Allen

Boris Onishchenko, the Soviet Union's reigning world champion in the modern pentathlon, was disqualified during the Olympic competition today for using a wired electronic epee. He was found to have a piece of wire concealed on his epee to trigger the electronic scoring machine.

Onishchenko, 38, a teacher from Kiev, was disqualified after a protest by Jeremy Fox, the experienced British modern pentathlete. Fox believed that Onishchenko was recording "hits" without his epee touching his opponent. Earlier another member of the British team, Adrian Parker, had also had a dubious hit from the Russian recorded against him. After Fox's vehement protest, the fencing officials took away Onishchenko's weapon to examine it. The Russian continued to fence with another epee until the officials met to decide that he should be disqualified.

Later Carl Schwende, chief of discipline in fencing, said: "The weapon had obviously been tampered with. Someone had wired it in such a way that it would score a winning hit without making contact."

Onishchenko protested that the epee was not his. But as his disqualification became inevitable, an official was heard to say: "This is a terrible thing for our sport."

When disqualified, the Russian had looked dumbfounded but had made no comment. The jury of appeal met for more than two hours before formally confirming that Onishchenko had been thrown out of the Games.

Last April, Onishchenko was a member of the winning Soviet team which competed at Crystal Palace and there I saw him warmly greeted by the British modern pentathletes, including Fox, all of whom have a high regard for a master of his sport, who has been on his national team since 1966.

While the British competitors, including an angry but distressed Fox, consider whether their idol has feet of clay, reporters can comment accurately, if sardonically, that the Soviet Union's team handbook – presumably because of the glue used – is the only evil-smelling one of any of the dozen littering the press rooms.

The expulsion of Onishchenko is likely to bring calls for even closer scrutiny of fencers' swords. There is no record of an Olympic fencer cheating using mechanical or electrical devices to produce a fake hit.

A judge examines Boris Onischenko's épée at the 1976 Olympics. Onishchenko was disqualified from the modern pentathlon for tampering with his weapon.

'Drug cheat' Johnson stripped of gold

Men's 100 metres | Athletics

Seoul, 1988

FROM JOHN GOODBODY, SPORTS NEWS CORRESPONDENT

Ben Johnson, the Canadian sprinter who won the Olympic Games 100 metres in a world record time on Saturday, has been stripped of his gold medal after failing a drugs test. He was also formally disqualified from the Seoul Olympics by the executive board of the International Olympic Committee.

Miss Michèle Verdier, the IOC spokeswoman, said that a urine sample taken from Johnson had contained traces of a banned anabolic steroid. The IOC said that the medical commission had listened to arguments by the Canadians and Johnson that the drug might have been administered by a third party. But she added that the urine sample was "not consistent with such a claim". Señor Juan Antonio Samaranch, the president of the IOC, said: "This has been a blow for the Olympic Games and the Olympic movement."

Carl Lewis of the United States, Johnson's great rival, is now almost certain to take the gold for the 100 metres. Linford Christie of Britain, who was third, would take the silver, and Calvin Smith, also of the US, the bronze.

At a meeting in Seoul of the International Amateur Athletics Federation, it was decided to suspend Johnson for two years from all international competition. In Ottawa, the Canadian Government announced that Johnson had been suspended for life from participating in Canadian national sports teams.

The substance found in Johnson's urine was reported to be stanozolol, which is related in structure to the male hormone testosterone and is used to increase muscle bulk, strength and power. Sources close to Johnson said he would appeal against the finding on the ground that the urine test had been mishandled.

Mr Larry Heiderbrecht, his business manager, said: "Ben is obviously sick at the news and will appeal. He is shattered." Asked whether he was tearful, Mr Heiderbrecht said: "He does not show much emotion." He added that Johnson had been tested more than any other athlete in the world. "He does not take drugs. It is obvious that something very strange has been happening."

Drug-taking in athletics is a widely recognised problem, and in the past 10 years dozens of athletes have been banned from the sport for it. Rumours are rife that countless more athletes are taking drugs. However, no other drugs case in athletics history compares with this.

Johnson had dazzled the world with his performance in the final, breaking his own world record with a time of 9.79s, and easily beating Lewis into second place.

Opposite Top – Ben Johnson, of Canada, leads the field in the 100 metres ahead of the American Carl Lewis (right) and Linford Christie (second right), of Britain, at Seoul 1988. The three men finished in that order before Johnson was disqualified for failing a drugs test.

Opposite Bottom – Johnson looks over at rival Lewis (far right) at the finish of the 100 metres in Seoul 1988. Johnson won ahead of Lewis, with Christie (second right) in third and Calvin Smith (second left) fourth.

Hurricane Florence in flow

Women's 100 metres | Athletics

Seoul, 1988

From Pat Butcher, Athletics Correspondent

Florence Griffith Joyner yesterday won the women's 100 metres gold medal with a run so dazzling it beat the Olympic record by 0.43s and so easy she could afford to break into a huge smile 30 metres before the finish.

With her 10.54s, Griffith Joyner finished four metres in front of Evelyn Ashford, the champion four years ago, and the East German Heike Drechsler. It was a stunning, showbusiness performance from this woman with the vast wardrobe of running costumes, the maquillage ever ready for a photocall, and the long, multi-coloured fingernails for the television close-ups.

Hurricane Florence, who broke the world record in the US trials, won by the biggest margin of victory since electrical timing was introduced. And, like Ben Johnson the previous day, she had prevented the incumbent, in this case Ashford, retaining her title. Ashford, was second in 10.83s and Drechsler third in 10.85s.

"I was smiling because I was so confident," Griffith Joyner said afterwards. "I felt that I had won the race. I wasn't interested in the world record, I just wanted to win." Ashford responded with an enigmatic: "There's no female who can beat her and maybe no male." Drechsler looked her usual happy self.

Griffith Joyner left her coach Bob Kersee only a few weeks ago over a managerial dispute. He had been instrumental in transforming her from a 'lazy bank clerk' (in her own words) to an Olympic champion.

NOTE: Griffith Joyner died in her sleep in 1998, at the age of 38, having suffered an epileptic seizure. She was dogged by suspicions of doping but never failed a test and her world records in the 100 metres and 200 metres still stand.

Florence Griffith Joyner, of the United States, celebrates as she storms away to win gold in the 200 metres in Seoul, in which she also broke the world record.

Jones loses 'criminal' decision

Men's light-middleweight | Boxing

Seoul, 1988

FROM JOHN GOODBODY

Roy Jones, the American light-middleweight, lost the most controversial decision of the Olympic boxing tournament. Even his opponent, Park Si-hun, lifted Jones off the canvas when the judging was announced, apparently to acknowledge that the wrong man had been awarded gold.

Heinz Birkle, a West German who sits on the executive committee of world governing body, AIBA, said: "It's criminal."

Jones, aged 19, had appeared to outclass the South Korean. But while the judges from the Soviet Union and Hungary voted him the winner by four points – in amateur boxing terms, a landslide – those from Uganda, Uruguay and Morocco had the Korean just in front. Frank Hendry, a leading British official, described the decision as "shocking; 60-56 was about right".

Anwar Chowdhry, president of the International Amateur Boxing Association (AIBA), also said that the decision was unfair and the international governing body promptly awarded the Val Barker trophy to Jones as the outstanding boxer of the tournament.

However, the AIBA was unable to intervene because it had abandoned the system of the jury of appeal being able to overrule the decision of the judges.

Jones was commendably restrained. "I am sick. So anyone would be who has been robbed," he said.

Seung-Youn Kim, the president of the Korean Amateur Boxing Association, denied that the decision was unjust. "I cannot understand why foreigners have a prejudice against Korea. It is a disgrace to Koreans," he said.

South Korea's Park Si-hun (left) throws a left jab at Roy Jones in the gold medal bout of the light middleweight division at the 1988 Olympics. Park controversially won on points.

Drug test problem for Ireland's Smith

Women's swimming

Atlanta, 1996

By Craig Lord (1998)

Michelle Smith, the controversial swimmer who became Ireland's greatest sporting heroine when she won three Olympic titles in Atlanta in 1996, faces possible suspension after a drug test problem.

The Irish Swimming Association has been informed by FINA, the sport's international ruling body, of the drug test. The sample is believed to have been produced when out-of-competition testers called on Smith unannounced early this year, and to have been analysed at a European laboratory.

Smith, 28, from Rathcoole, near Dublin, may now request that the "B" sample taken for the drug test be analysed to confirm or annul the result of the "A" sample. It is believed that the drug test did not involve a specific banned substance, but a test may be deemed a failure if there is evidence that a sample has been tampered with.

The nature of the drug test will determine the suspension that Smith faces. FINA rules allow for a suspension of up to four years for the most serious abuses.

Peter Lennon, Smith's solicitor, said last night: "She has not failed a drugs test within the meaning of the rules." Asked what he meant, Mr Lennon replied: "Have you ever known an athlete to have been suspended for taking a drug that is not itemised or particularised? Have you ever known an athlete to have been suspended for interfering with a sample, as is alleged here?"

At the Games two years ago, Smith won the 400 metres individual medley, the 400 metres freestyle and the 200 metres individual medley. She took bronze in the 200 metres butterfly. Her achievements were tarnished by unsubstantiated rumours of drug use, which she always denied.

Her extraordinary improvement in form, which came late in her career and catapulted her from relative anonymity, coincided with her relationship with Erik de Bruin, the coach who became her husband. They met at the Olympic Games in 1992 when Smith was ranked outside the best 50 swimmers in the world.

NOTE: Smith was later given a four-year ban for manipulating a drug sample but was allowed to keep her Olympic medals.

Michelle Smith answers questions from the press amidst a drugs controversy following her triumphs in 1996.

Greek stars suspended over drug tests

Athletics

Athens, 2004

FROM DAVID WALSH, CHIEF SPORTS WRITER

The Greek Olympic Committee has suspended the country's two greatest stars, the sprinters Kostas Kenteris and Ekaterini Thanou, from the Olympic Games in Athens. The athletes' banishment from the event is due to be confirmed tomorrow at a meeting of the International Olympic Committee (IOC) disciplinary meeting.

The Greeks voted by a five-to-one majority to suspend the athletes and their controversial coach, Christos Tzekos. After missing a drug test in Chicago at the beginning of the week, Kenteris and Thanou missed a second test at the athletes' Olympic village on Thursday evening. The latest missed test occurred in circumstances so suspicious that it seems certain that the pair will be expelled.

Kenteris's lawyer, Michalis Dimitrakopoulos, insists the athletes have done nothing wrong. "They have nothing to hide," he said. "All these allegations will eventually collapse." But the weight of evidence against them is formidable. Drug testers tried to obtain urine samples from Kenteris, the current Olympic 200 metres champion, and Thanou, the Olympic 100 metres silver medallist, at the Olympic village on Thursday evening, but the athletes were not in their rooms.

They had, apparently, gone to their respective homes in Athens to pick up some personal belongings. Frantic efforts to contact them by phone and get them back to the village lasted for almost six hours. According to their coach, they were at his house in the seaside suburb of Goyfada and learned about the intended drug test only late at night. In their midnight rush to return, Kenteris claimed to have crashed his motorbike, injuring himself and Thanou. So far, no witness to the crash has come forward. No other vehicle was involved, there was no call to the emergency services or involvement of the police.

A nurse at the hospital where the pair were treated has claimed that when Kenteris and Thanou turned up, they showed no outward signs of having been involved in a road crash. Suspicion that they had deliberately tried to avoid their drug tests led to yesterday's meeting of the Greek Olympic Committee.

NOTE: The pair ended up withdrawing from the Games. They later accepted charges relating to missed drug tests and both were given two-year bans.

Opposite Top – *Kostas Kenteris (right) and his lawyer prepare to give a statement after the Greek athlete missed a drugs test at the 2004 Games.*

Opposite Bottom – *Ekaterini Thanou (far right) is questioned by the press about her missed test.*

Israeli athletes killed on Olympics' darkest day

Munich, 1972

FROM OUR FOREIGN STAFF

All nine of the Israeli hostages seized by Palestinian militants at the Olympic village in Munich yesterday were killed during a gun battle between the terrorists and West German security forces at an airport near Munich.

Four of the militants and a policeman died in the shooting at Fürstenfeldbruck military airport where the Palestinians were attempting to escape with their hostages.

A helicopter pilot was also reported to have been seriously wounded. A West German government spokesman said that marksmen opened fire on the terrorists after helicopters carrying the group and their hostages landed at the airport.

Because of the darkness, the marksmen did not hit all of their targets and the terrorists then turned their weapons on the helicopters.

Eyewitnesses at the airport said that a Boeing 707 of the West German airline Lufthansa was waiting on the airstrip as the helicopters bringing the terrorists and their hostages from the Olympic village landed. As the hostages and their captors walked towards it, the marksmen, hidden in the darkness behind the airliner, opened fire. The Palestinians fired back, and the exchange of fire continued for several minutes.

Herr Bruno Merk, the Bavarian minister of the interior, said one of the helicopters was blown up by a grenade. The mayor of Munich, Herr Kronawitter,

A team of snipers take up position in the Olympic Village at Munich 1972 whilst pro-Palestine terrorists hold Israeli athletes hostage.

said that three other Palestinians were still at large. The mayor himself had just left the airport. He described the scene there as "terrible".

The day before, the terrorists had killed two Israelis when they occupied the team's headquarters. Because of this, the Olympic Games were suspended. The announcement was made by Mr Avery Brundage, the outgoing President of the International Olympic Committee. "The Olympic peace has been broken by an act of assassination by criminal terrorists. The whole civilised world condemns this barbaric crime, this horror," he said.

The postponement decision reversed an earlier announcement that the Games would continue as planned. Mrs Golda Meir, the Israel Prime Minister, had asked the Olympic authorities for a suspension.

The attack on the Israel team headquarters had begun shortly after 5am. A telephone engineer who was testing equipment nearby said that he saw several men climbing over the 7ft fence around the village. Because they were carrying sports bags, he assumed they were athletes who were sneaking back to the village secretively after a night on the town. Twenty minutes later a series of shots was heard and the alarm raised. An Israeli journalist in the village said that the terrorists had entered the team's headquarters and opened fire with sub-machine guns at Israelis as they lay in their beds.

Moshe Weinberg, aged 33, a coach, had been killed as he tried to escape. The other dead man was Joseph Romano, an Israeli weightlifter. His body was later placed outside the building by the militants.

The terrorists, members of the extremist Palestinian group Black September, threatened to kill all their Israeli hostages if 200 Palestinian prisoners held in Israel were not released. Throughout the day they then set a number of deadlines. When the group's demands were not met, the aircraft was drawn up at their request ready for take-off.

A pro-Palestine militant peers out of the apartment where a group of Israeli athletes are being held hostage.

INNOVATORS

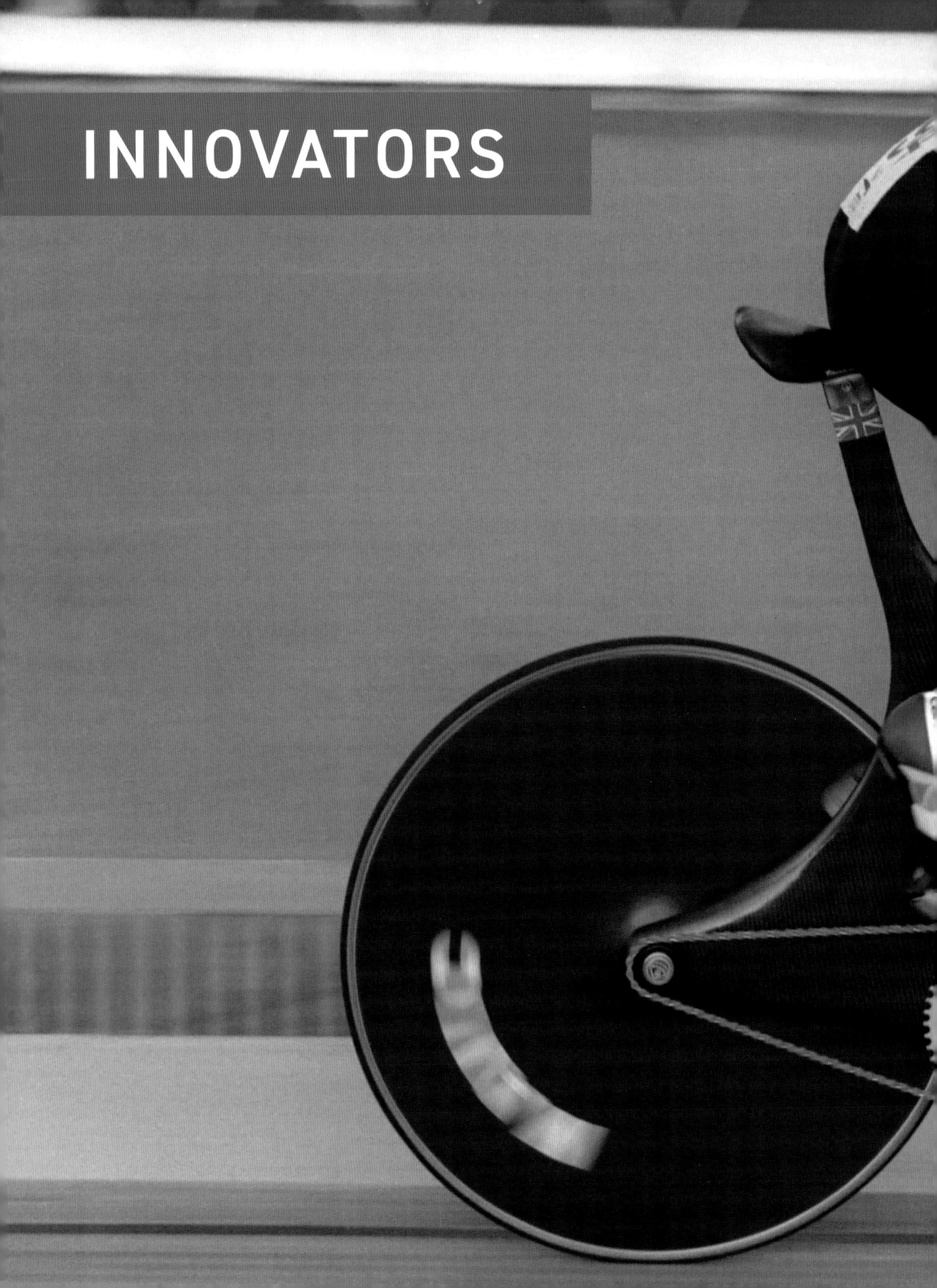

Fosbury's 'flop' transformed high jump

Men's high jump | Athletics

Mexico City, 1968

Dick Fosbury took the Olympic high jump title with his novel style, which enraptured the Mexican crowd and revolutionised the event for years to come. With a technique nicknamed 'The Fosbury Flop', the American, after leaping upwards, had his back facing the bar, instead of his chest in the popular style of the straddle.

But Fosbury still struggled to take the gold medal ahead of his teammate Ed Caruthers. They were the only athletes left in the competition when the height was raised to 2.24 metres – the remaining 10 finalists, as well as Caruthers, used the straddle. Both Americans had two failures at this height. Fosbury was the first to jump on their third and final attempt. For almost two minutes, he rocked backwards and forwards, repeatedly clenching and unclenching his fists, focusing on the attempt, which seemed to everyone a trial of the efficacy of the 'Flop'. Finally, he broke into his long and speedy run, took off, and narrowly cleared the bar. The spectators were ecstatic. It then seemed inevitable that Caruthers would fail. And he did. Fosbury then had three unsuccessful tries at breaking the world record of 2.28 metres of Valeriy Brumel of the Soviet Union.

Fosbury's success and that of Canadian Debbie Brill, who employed a similar technique, which was dubbed 'The Brill Bend', have been copied for years by other jumpers seeking greater heights. Fosbury had a long, curved run to build momentum, taking off from his right foot, the leg farther away from the bar. He propelled himself over the bar on his back, landing headfirst. The higher the bar, the farther away from it Fosbury took off. The positioning of the body meant there was a much lower centre of gravity in flight. This technique had only become feasible in recent years when the foam rubber pit or thick mattress had replaced sand as a landing area. The style was deemed legal because the rules just stated that a competitor must take off from one leg not two.

Fosbury, 21, from Oregon State University, took some time to evolve the technique. He had been unsuccessful at school using the conventional straddle, which had superseded the scissors, western roll, and the Eastern cut-off in popularity during the twentieth century. He reverted to the scissors, in which the jumper is upright throughout the technique but then Fosbury began to lie backwards over the bar and the Flop was born. By 1965 he had cleared 2.01 metres and then in 1967, 2.10 metres, but this height was unlikely to make him a contender for the U.S. Olympic team given the depth in American strength in the event.

However, he achieved 2.14 metres indoors in January 1968, and in the summer, retained his National Collegiate Athletic Association title, getting him a place in the Olympic try-outs. The Americans decided to have secondary trials near South Lake Tahoe to see how athletes would cope with the altitude they were to face here. Fosbury qualified, clearing his path to an Olympic gold medal.

By John Goodbody

Dick Fosbury clears the bar using a technique that revolutionised the high jump.

Beamon destroys field with landmark leap

Men's long jump | Athletics

Mexico City, 1968

FROM JOHN LOVESEY

In the midst of all the demonstrations on the winners rostrum, Bob Beamon's victory in the Olympic long jump with a first leap of 29ft 2½in must rank as one of the most devastating and crushing wins of these Games. How long it will be before this new world record is broken is anybody's guess, but it is a fair bet that nobody will ever better it except in the thin air of Mexico City.

Beamon's leap killed his opponents, and even seemed to stun himself. He only tried one more jump when he achieved a moderate 26ft ½in. His first jump, even despite the advantage of competing in air which creates far less resistance, was a mammoth athletic feat, in which his speed down the runway, his timing and leap up and out must have reached a perfection that he may never quite manage again. "Beamon didn't jump," said one American, who had to keep checking his metric conversion tables, "He flew."

Before the competition his rivals Ralph Boston, Lynn Davies and Igor Ter-Ovanesyan had met together and one of them had said, only in half jest, that they should at all costs avoid making Beamon angry or he would "go into orbit".

When Beamon was asked whether he had been angry in the long jump final, he replied he had only been frightened. "I figured the pressure was on me and I knew I'd have to go one hundred per cent."

The effect on Lynn Davies, who won the gold medal in Tokyo, was near-catastrophic. "I can't do 29 feet 2 inches, and all I was interested in was the gold," he said later. "I knew I couldn't do that much." This was despite the fact that when rain fell, as it has here, with devastating effectiveness on occasions, clearing the stands of fans, a slim British hope remained that perhaps Davies could repeat his 1964 Olympic victory, achieved in the rain.

Instead, after Beamon's opening leap, Davies turned to Ralph Boston and sadly confessed, "I can't go on after a jump like that." The effect was clear in his own first jump, when he almost ran through the landing pit, recording a leap of a little over 21ft which hardly compares to his best performance of 27ft this year. His second jump was better, half an inch over 26ft, and then he had a no-jump. Even if legitimate, it would have clearly made no difference.

Bob Beamon launches his world-record long jump at the 1968 Games in Mexico City. The record stood until 1991.

Elfin Olga casts a magical spell

Women's gymnastics

Munich, 1972

Few Olympians have entranced the public as much as the Soviet gymnast Olga Korbut, whose performances at the 1972 Games brought unprecedented interest in the sport. When she finished only seventh in the all-around competition, having fluffed her routine on the asymmetric bars, she burst into tears. Around the world many television viewers apparently cried with her, just as they rejoiced when she later took two individual golds, in the beam and floor exercise events, along with a silver in the uneven bars.

Those Games were the first with saturation coverage of many events at peak viewing time in Europe and the response of the public to the elfin-like Korbut was extraordinary. Soviet soldiers wanted pin-up photographs; American matrons wanted to mother her; and in Britain, clubs were overwhelmed by girls wanting to be gymnasts.

Korbut was popular precisely because she erred at crucial moments. When a spectator ran forward with a bouquet after the blunder on the bars that year, she gave overt expression to every spectator's sympathy. Korbut became a celebrity, touring the world to meet people such as US President Richard Nixon, tottering under pressure over the Watergate Scandal. He told her: "I have always been impressed with your ability to land on your feet."

By John Goodbody

Olga Korbut during her gold medal-winning balance beam routine at the Munich Olympics. The Soviet athlete won three golds at the 1972 Games.

Boardman ends Britain's 84-year wait

Men's individual pursuit |
Track cycling

Barcelona, 1992

FROM PETER BRYAN

Chris Boardman won Britain's first gold medal of the 1992 Olympic Games here yesterday. Riding his show-stopping Lotus bike, Boardman swept to a magnificent victory in the 4,000 metres pursuit final and gave Britain its first individual Olympic track cycling champion since 1908.

The spectators packing the Horta Velodrome did not need the electronic clock to confirm Boardman's triumph. They thrilled to his relentless chase of the world champion, Jens Lehmann, from the start and Boardman, aged 23, caught the German after 3,700 metres to ensure the race did not go the full distance.

"I never expected to catch Lehmann and thought the race would be a fight to the line," Boardman said. "It was a nice surprise when, just before the three-kilometre mark, I had him in my sights."

Boardman, who lives on the Wirral, confessed to nerves as he prepared for the two races of his life. "As the day went on, I was getting more nervous – to the extent that I was almost physically sick," he said. "I remember telling my helpers that I never, never wanted to be in this situation again."

Boardman's aerodynamic bike has seen him go faster on an outdoor track than anyone. There are no official pursuit records but his times in Barcelona are acknowledged as such by his rivals. He always maintained that the carbon-fibre frame would make the difference between finishing third or winning the gold medal. Before the final, the German camp accepted that their man would be riding for silver.

"You have the best man here at the Games and also the best machine," one official said. "Britain has set new pursuiting standards and there will now be a rush by other countries to find an answer." Boardman said: "The Lotus bike was obviously significant otherwise I wouldn't have been using it. It will be developed further next year, I understand."

But he would not be drawn on his future. "I am normally a person who makes lots of plans, but I am looking at going for Francesco Moser's world one-hour record." It was in London, 84 years ago, that a British cyclist last won an individual Olympic gold medal and 1920 when Britain last won any cycling event. Harry Ryan and Thomas Lance took the 2,000 metres tandem title.

British track cyclist Chris Boardman salutes the crowd after winning the individual pursuit at Barcelona 1992, where he won gold on his revolutionary Lotus bike.

Pistorius rounds out a golden summer

Men's T44 400 metres | Athletics
London Paralympics, 2012

By Andrew Longmore, for *The Sunday Times*

Oscar Pistorius arrived at the Olympic Stadium in London for the final time last night with his pride and his reputation in need of a little polish. He left with his precious T44 400 metres title safely retained for another four years and with a broad smile on his face.

The South African must know this part of London as well as any East End cabbie after making his Olympic debut more than five weeks ago and then returning to shoulder the profoundly different pressure of being the world's highest-profile Paralympian. If not quite performing a lap of redemption, the Bladerunner needed to remind a few of the 80,000 people inside the stadium of his athletic talent. By the end of his time at the Olympics, Pistorius had achieved the almost impossible feat of being just another runner.

Fittingly, his last hurrah was kept to the end of nine days of athletics stretching from early morning to late night and across a bewildering array of categories and classifications, more than 170 in total. The crowd cheered his every move from the moment he stepped on to the track to the final farewell wave.

One lane to his outside was Alan Oliveira, the 200 metres champion; three lanes away Blake Leeper, an old rival. On paper, there could be no doubt. Pistorius was the only runner in the field to have broken 50 seconds.

It was a build-up worthy of a prize fight, though the interminable wait on the blocks would have tested the patience of the most experienced athlete. Pistorius made no mistake and by halfway the race had turned into a procession. At the line, the South African raised both hands to the heavens and received the congratulations of all his rivals. His time of 46.68s was a Paralympic world record. Leeper, in second, was nearly four seconds behind. It was some performance, some climax.

"This is the 11th time I've run on this track and so I wanted to give the crowd something to remember the Paralympics by," Pistorius said. "I'm quite tired now, but for the first time in my life I could hear the crowd as I was coming down the straight. Usually, I'm too focused to hear but it was an amazing feeling. I wanted to give my best."

NOTE: Pistorius's legacy was ruined when he was found guilty of the murder of his girlfriend Reeva Steenkamp in 2018. He was sentenced to 13 years in prison.

Opposite Top – *Oscar Pistorius on his way to winning gold in the T44 400 metres at the London 2012 Paralympics.*

Opposite Bottom – *Pistorius reaches to take the baton from South Africa team-mate Arnu Fourie during the T42/ T46 4 x 100 metres relay at the 2012 Paralympics.*

Adams breaks boxing's glass ceiling

Women's flyweight | Boxing

London, 2012

BY RON LEWIS AT THE EXCEL ARENA

Nicola Adams fought her way into the record books yesterday to become the first women's Olympic boxing champion and give the sport its own Jessica Ennis. Boxing could not have a better poster girl, according to the Great Britain performance director, Rob McCracken.

"She is always smiling, she's the type of person that you always want to be around," he said after she won the flyweight title with a convincing victory over Ren Cancan of China. Adams, 29, from Leeds, was beaming as she celebrated her success at the ExCel arena.

"I can't believe the support I've had. The whole of Great Britain has got behind women's boxing," she said. "I'd like to think that I could inspire some kids to do what I have done and maybe take it to the next level. When I started, there weren't really any other girls boxing, but I loved it from the first time I did it."

One of her former trainers, Fred Gummerson, 80, said that he had watched the fight yesterday with "a couple of tears in my eyes". He initially refused to let her train at his gym in Cudworth, near Barnsley. "When she came to us, I said I'd never have a woman in my gym," admitted Mr Gummerson, who has trained 19 national champions. "I didn't believe in women boxing. But after I saw Nicola sparring with my lads – good lads – I was totally sold," he said. She had boxed "absolutely beautifully" in the final, he added.

Before becoming a funded athlete in the Olympic squad, Adams made a living as a fitness instructor, giving boxing classes and supplementing her income as an extra on television soap operas such as Coronation Street and Emmerdale. She has also played a boxer in the ITV sitcom My Parents are Aliens. "I don't have the time to do that now, but it is something I'd like to go back into," she said. "In Coronation Street and Emmerdale, I'm mainly in the background in the pub or in the street. I haven't been given a line yet." First on her mind last night, though, was dinner. "Nando's," she said. "I'll have chicken pitta, medium heat, with chips." Do you drink? she was asked. "Why not?" For a few weeks at least, making the weight is not an issue.

Right – Team GB's Nicola Adams lands a blow on Stoyka Petrova, of Bulgaria, during their flyweight quarter-final at London 2012.

Opposite – Adams celebrates beating Ren Cancan at the ExCeL Arena, London, to become the Olympics' first female boxing champion.

AGAINST
THE ODDS

Eyser wins triple gold with wooden leg

Men's gymnastics

St Louis, 1904

George Eyser won a remarkable three Olympic gold medals and three other medals in one day, despite having a prosthetic leg.

Eyser, who had his leg amputated after being hit by a train in his youth, triumphed in the parallel bars, the vault and the rope-climbing event.

He won silver in the pommel horse, bronze in the horizontal bar and silver as part of the United States team competing in the combined event.

Born in Germany, Eyser emigrated to the US with his family as a 14-year-old. Originally based in Denver, they moved to St Louis, where Eyser, 34, combines his athletic training with a job as a book-keeper. He is a member of the Concordia Turnverein, a renowned gymnastics club in St Louis.

An incredibly determined individual, Eyser also competed in the triathlon in the athletics events at the Games, finishing in last place.

By Robert Dineen

George Eyser (centre) with his Concordia Turnverein gymnastics team from St Louis. Eyser won three golds at the 1904 Games despite competing with a prosthetic leg.

Abrahams shocks the Americans

Men's 100 metres | Athletics

Paris, 1924

From Our Special Correspondent

The crowd at the Olympic Stadium was probably less than half the attendance of yesterday, the cheaper seats, which on Sunday were thronged with holidaymakers, being almost entirely empty. There were, however, 25,000 or 30,000 people present, which in anything smaller than a modern stadium would make a great assemblage, and those who were present had plenty of thrills.

In the semi-final heats of the 100 metres, the Briton Harold Abrahams, starting very badly, but running with amazing strength at the finish, again equalled the Olympic record with 10⅗s. Until his graduation last summer, Abrahams was the president of the Cambridge University Athletics Club, having left his role as lieutenant in the British Army to take up a degree.

In what we hoped would be the thrill of the day, Abrahams ran a fine race in the final and was the first to reach the tape, but he could do no more than equal for the third time the Olympic record. Jackson Scholz, the American who had been heavily fancied to win gold, was second and Arthur Porritt, of New Zealand, third.

Britain's Harold Abrahams wins the 100 metres at the Paris Games in 1924 ahead of Jackson Scholz (second right), of the United States, and New Zealand's Arthur Porritt (far left) in third.

ABRAHAMS

SCHOLZ   PADDOCK

OLYMPIQUES DE 1924
VÉE DU 100ᵐ ABRAHAMS 1ᵉʳ

Korea's rebel with a cause

Men's marathon | Athletics

Berlin, 1936

Most athletes revel in the euphoria of winning an Olympic title and standing at the victory ceremony as their national flag is raised and their anthem played. However, emotions were mixed in 1936 for the marathon winner Sohn Kee-chung, who was born Korean but, in Berlin, officially represented Japan, then occupying his country.

Sohn bowed his head to signify his protest at being listed as Japanese, later telling journalists he was Korean. When a newspaper in his homeland published a picture of Sohn with the Rising Sun on his tracksuit scratched out, Japan reacted with fury. The newspaper was shut for nearly a year.

Sohn built his stamina as a boy after one of his teachers told him to fill the pockets of his trousers with sand and put stones in his rucksack to make running harder. In November 1935, he set a world marathon record of 2hr 26min 42s, and the following year qualified for the Japanese team in the trials in Tokyo. Although given the Japanese name of Kitei Son, the Kanji equivalent of his name, Sohn always signed his name in Korean and drew little maps alongside his signature to show where his homeland was in relation to Japan.

In 1988, when Seoul hosted the Olympics, Sohn was selected to carry the torch into the stadium and his joy was evident as he pranced along the track.

By John Goodbody

Korea's Sohn Kee-chung carries the Olympic flame into the stadium during the opening ceremony of the 1988 Games in Seoul. The 76-year-old won the marathon at the Berlin Olympics 52 years earlier, when he was forced to compete for Japan.

Pool shark stars on one leg

Men's water polo

Los Angeles, 1932 and Berlin, 1936

The most celebrated Olympic amputee was the Hungarian Olivér Halassy, who was injured when his right foot was crushed in a traffic accident, but still won two water polo gold medals in the Games and the European 1,500 metres freestyle title.

The injury was so severe that the rest of the leg below the knee had to be removed. Despite that surgery, he was regarded as the outstanding player in the 1936 Games. John Atkinson, Britain's national performance director for Paralympic swimming, hails the achievements of Halassy as "amazing, just astonishing. In swimming he would have had the disadvantage right from the start when he was unable to drive off the blocks. Even more significant was that in a 1,500 metres race, there are 29 turns and he would have been unable to get a proper push-off from the wall and would not have been able to kick underwater. He would also have had no balance in his stroke."

His inability to use his legs properly would also have hindered him in water polo. Atkinson explains: "Players use their legs to get momentum, when they chase after the ball or an opponent. In addition, they need to drive from the legs to rise up out of the water when they are passing or shooting."

Born in 1909 in Haltmayer, just north of Budapest, Halassy first competed in the Olympics in Amsterdam, where Hungary took the silver medal. His swimming career, which included 25 Hungarian individual titles, climaxed at the 1931 European championships in Paris, where he won the 1,500 metres in 20min 49s.

With his sturdy physique, stamina and ball-handling skills, he was outstanding as a water polo half-back. The other leading player was János "Jim" Németh. At the 1932 Olympics, Németh scored nine times and Halassy seven, as the team racked up 30 goals, conceding just two. The 1936 contest in Berlin was much tighter, with Hungary and the highly-trained Germans, cheered on by capacity crowds, each winning six matches. The rivals drew 2-2 when they met, but Hungary took gold because of a better overall goal average. In 1946 Halassy, an auditor, was shot dead by an occupying Soviet soldier as he returned by taxi to his Budapest home. His wife gave birth to their third child a few days later.

By John Goodbody

Olivér Halassy (third right) with Hungary's gold medal-winning water polo team in 1936. Halassy excelled in his sport despite having only one leg.

Soldier survives grenade to triumph

Men's 25-metre rapid-fire pistol | Shooting

London, 1948

Since the Second World War, only one disabled competitor has won an Olympic gold medal — the Hungarian Károly Takács.

Born in Budapest in 1910, Takacs joined the army and became a superb marksman with the pistol. In 1936, he was denied a place in the Olympic team because he was a sergeant and the Hungarians only picked commissioned officers. Takács won the 1938 European title but shortly afterwards, while on manoeuvres, a faulty hand grenade shattered his shooting hand. His sporting career seemed over.

However, Takács, undaunted, continued training, now using his left hand. In 1948, the Olympic shooting events were held at Bisley in Surrey and the favourite for the rapid-fire pistol was Argentina's Carlos Sáenz Valiente, the world champion and world record holder. When he asked Takács why he was in London, the Hungarian replied: "I am here to learn."

The rapid-fire event entailed firing 60 shots at man-sized black targets 25 metres away. The targets had scoring areas that were swung into position at intervals of eight, six and four seconds. At the halfway point, Valiente led but then Takács, who had scored 286 in his first 30 shots, became increasingly accurate, gradually overhauling his rival. The Hungarian finally got 294 points for his last batch of 30 attempts to total 580 and take the gold medal. The Argentine had thought he would win with his own total of 571, one more than his world record. On the podium, he turned to Takács, congratulated him and said: "I think you have learnt enough."

Tom Redhead, the British head pistol coach at the 2012 Olympics, has hailed the performance. "It was a hell of an accomplishment. It must have taken tremendous perseverance and strength of will to come back after an accident like that. He would have had to teach himself to acquire the muscle memory with his left hand that he had when using his right."

Neither was his victory in London the end. Four years later he retained his title in Helsinki as the first rapid-fire pistol shooter to take two Olympic gold medals, this time by just one point from both his compatriot Szilárd Kun, in second, and the Romanian bronze medallist Gheorghe Lichiardopol. When Takács retired, as a lieutenant-colonel, he had won 38 Hungarian titles. He died in 1976.

By John Goodbody

Hungary's Károly Takács at London 1948, where he won shooting gold competing with his weaker left hand. The army officer's right hand had been shattered in a grenade explosion.

Teenage allrounder defies all logic

Men's decathlon | Athletics

London, 1948

What was extraordinary about the victory of American Bob Mathias at the 1948 Games was not just that he had taken up the decathlon that spring but that he was only 17, the youngest athletics gold medallist in Olympic history in an event that demands experience and thorough preparation.

Four years later in Helsinki, Mathias retained his title and retired unbeaten. Yet, as a boy in the town of Tulare, California, he was often sickly, suffering from anaemia. His father, a doctor, encouraged his four children to take part in athletic events and by the age of 12 Bob could clear 1.67m in the high jump. In the spring of 1948, he entered the decathlon at the Southern Pacific AAU championships, though he had never competed in the long jump, javelin or 1,500 metres, and had not tried the pole vault. He won so easily that he qualified for the Olympic trials, at which he also triumphed.

It rained on the second day of the Games and the competition fell behind schedule. In the discus, Mathias launched a huge throw but, in the gloom, officials could not find its mark in the turf. He eventually accepted a 44m mark, still the best of the day. When the javelin started, cars were driven on to the track for their headlights to illuminate the field. Mathias kept his lead. The 1,500 metres was run at 10.30pm and Mathias dragged himself to victory.

By John Goodbody

Opposite – Bob Mathias, the 17-year-old American, competes in the discus during his triumphant decathlon campaign at the 1948 Olympics in London.

Below – Mathias (right) competes in the 110 metres hurdles event as part of the decathlon. Alongside him are (left) Oto Rebula of Yugoslavia and (centre) Iceland's Orn Clausen.

Coachman raises bar in racism battle

Women's high jump | Athletics

London, 1948

Alice Coachman was the first Black American woman to win an Olympic gold medal, triumphing over Britain's Dorothy Tyler in the high jump at the 1948 Games. When she returned to her native Georgia, segregation marred the celebrations, though her success would play a part in breaking down race barriers in the United States.

In 1952, Coca-Cola asked her to become the first Black female athlete to endorse a global consumer project. This status was a long way from her humble upbringing, the fifth of 10 children whose father worked as a plasterer. Coachman was an athletic child, excelling in the playground, always rising to the challenge when somebody said: "I bet you can't jump that".

She would usually prove them wrong, saying many years later: "It was competition, although [at that age] I wasn't to know." More formal athletic activities were later restricted because of the lack of training facilities in her part of town. Although the Black and White communities had separate educational and sports campuses, they were meant to be of the same standard. The reality was different.

Encouraged by a teacher and an aunt to develop her athletic talent, she trained on dirt roads, usually barefoot, round her hometown of Albany. In the 1940s, she won US titles in the sprints and high jump and was selected to go to the London Olympics. Tyler, aged only 16, had been desperately unlucky not to win the 1936 title, when the current countback rules were not in force. The same happened in 1948, when both Coachman and Tyler cleared 1.68 metres. But the Briton needed two efforts to achieve that height and Coachman one, so the American took gold. Coachman had been aided by sucking on a lemon rather than drinking water, saying: "It helped me when my mouth was dry. I liked to feel light so I didn't drink water in competition."

She did not realise she had won until she was summoned to the podium and saw the result on the scoreboard.

On her return to the United States, Coachman was one of the Black American athletes received at the White House by President Harry Truman. When she reached Atlanta in Georgia she was welcomed along the roads stretching almost 180 miles to Albany, where a civic celebration was held. She was congratulated by the mayor but he did not shake her hand. Neither did she speak publicly. She recalled many years later: "That was the way it was in 1948."

By John Goodbody

Alice Coachman, of the United States, clears the bar in the high jump competition at London 1948, where she became the first Black woman to win Olympic gold.

AN ACTION PHOTOGRAPH OF A. COACHMAN (U.S.A.), WHO
WON THE WOMEN'S HIGH JUMP AND BROKE THE OLYMPIC
RECORD WITH 5 FT. $6\frac{1}{8}$ IN.

Hartel blazes trail for polio victims

Individual Dressage | Equestrian

Helsinki, 1952

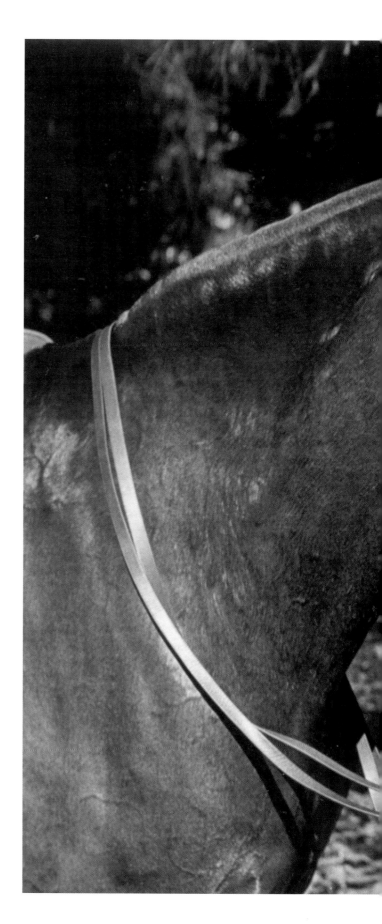

Denmark's Lis Hartel, a disabled competitor, earned admiration by taking part in two Olympic Games, winning equestrian medals in both. Her silver in 1952 was the first by any woman in any individual sport when in direct competition with men at the Olympics, and she was runner-up again in 1956.

Hartel had been Danish dressage champion in 1943 and 1944 but, that September, when pregnant with her second child, her body was paralysed by polio. As she tended her new-born child, she learned to crawl and finally walk, aided by crutches. Below the knee, her muscles remained paralysed.

Still Hartel was not finished. She insisted on riding, even though she had to be helped on to her horse, and in 1947 she began to compete once more in dressage. In 1952 she regained her Danish title and was selected for the Helsinki Olympics. The Ruskeasuo Arena was to witness one of the most extraordinary pieces in the entire tapestry of the Olympics.

Hartel, then 31, displayed astonishing control on her horse, Jubilee, taking silver behind a Swedish army officer, Henri Saint Cyr. As she was helped down from the horse, Saint Cyr ran to Hartel and helped her mount the podium for the medal ceremony. Britain's Carl Hester, a European champion, says: "I have never come across anyone who has taken part at that level with a disability like she had. It is inspirational."

By John Goodbody

Lis Hartel, of Denmark, with her horse Jubilee at Helsinki 1952. Hartel finished second in the dressage, becoming the first woman to win an Olympic medal competing against men.

Shepherd's son who conquered world

Men's marathon | Athletics

Rome, 1960 and Tokyo, 1964

With victories at both the 1960 and 1964 Olympic marathons, Abebe Bikila pioneered East African glory in long-distance running. His victory in Rome was a total surprise and marked the first of a series of triumphs by Ethiopians and Kenyans. He died aged only 41 from a brain haemorrhage. His funeral was attended by almost 100,000 people and the Ethiopian Emperor, Haile Selassie, announced a day of mourning.

Bikila was born the son of a shepherd, on August 7, 1932, the day of the Olympic marathon in Los Angeles. He joined the Imperial Bodyguard and his talent was discovered by Onni Niskanen, a Swedish coach hired to advise elite runners.

In Rome, Bikila (the name means "budding flower" in Amharic) could not find shoes to fit so he decided to run barefoot, something he did in training. He was entered with a best time of 2hr 21min 23s but athletics experts were sceptical because they doubted some African races were measured accurately. The marathon was held in the evening to protect the athletes from the heat, although the summer sun would have affected Bikila less than many other competitors.

He was in the lead group throughout, with his only real challenger in the second half being Rhadi Ben Abdesselam of Morocco. With just less than a mile to go, Bikila began to draw away from Rhadi and finished 25s clear in 2hr 15min 16.2s. The symbolism of an Ethiopian finishing in triumph at the Arch of Constantine, on the road the conquering Roman armies had marched, was lost on few people, given that the Italians had invaded Ethiopia 24 years previously.

When asked why he had run barefoot, Bikila replied: "I wanted to show that my country, Ethiopia, has always won with determination and heroism."

He needed an appendectomy only 40 days before the 1964 Tokyo marathon and his rivals could not believe he would be in peak form at the Games. They were wrong. He won by more than four minutes, which turned out to be the greatest margin of victory for 88 years, and he is one of only two men with two Olympic marathon golds.

By John Goodbody

Abebe Bikila wins the marathon at Rome 1960 in a breakthrough victory for African athletes.

Polio victim storms to triple crown

Women's 100 metres, 200 metres and 4 x 100 metres relay | Athletics

Rome, 1960

Few Olympic athletics champions have overcome such disabilities and illnesses in childhood as the sprinter Wilma Rudolph, who in 1960 became the first American female athlete to win three gold medals at the same Games. Her victories in Rome dented the wall of racism in American society.

Born prematurely, weighing little more than 2kg, she was the 20th of 22 children in a working-class family. For many years she could not walk unaided, let alone run. The hospital near her home in Clarksville, Tennessee, was for White people only and Wilma's mother had to tend her daughter through double pneumonia, chicken pox, mumps, measles and scarlet fever.

Aged four, she contracted polio. A doctor said Wilma would never walk again but her mother was determined to prove him wrong. With her left leg deformed, Wilma used crutches and had a brace fitted for three years. Twice a week she was driven to the nearest hospital that treated the Black community, 50 miles away. Her siblings took turns to massage Wilma's legs and when she was fully recovered, aged 12, she set her sights on sport.

Her athletic ability was uncovered at a summer track school at Tennessee State University, whose women's squad were known as the Tennessee Tigerbelles. At 16 she went to the Melbourne Olympics and won a bronze medal in the 100 metre relay, becoming one of the youngest track medallists in the history of the Games.

Wilma Rudolph (middle) anchors the United States to victory in the 4 x 100 metres relay at Rome 1960. It was one of three golds she won at the Games.

In July, 1960, she ran the 200 metres in 22.9 seconds, breaking the world record of the Australian Betty Cuthbert by 0.3s. Dorothy Hyman, Britain's most successful female sprinter, was to be Rudolph's chief rival at the Games. She recalls being reassured by the Irish athlete Maeve Kyle. "Maeve had seen her in training and said she was not that fast and was not as good as they were saying. What I do remember is how tall she seemed." Hyman, a relay gold medallist at the 1958 Commonwealth Games, was 1.69m compared with Rudolph's 1.81m.

In the 100 metre final Hyman got away well. "I was in front with about 40 yards to go. But Wilma came storming past me and I seemed to be taking two strides to her one."

Rudolph won in a wind-assisted 11.0 seconds, with Hyman second in 11.3 seconds. In the 200 metres Rudolph won by 0.4s. In the 100 metre relay the Tigerbelles, representing the United States en bloc and anchored by Rudolph, broke the world record in victory.

By John Goodbody

Wilma Rudolph on track before the 100 metres at Rome 1960, which she won along with the 200 metres and sprint relay.

Ageless Oerter overcomes agony

Men's discus | Athletics

Tokyo, 1964

The words of the American discus thrower Al Oerter resound down the ages. They are passed on as folklore from generation to generation of athletes.

Already twice the Olympic champion, he had to wear a surgical collar because of a neck injury in 1964 and then so badly damaged his ribs that he was strapped up like a mummy. Trailing in the final and defying the pain, he removed the collar and uttered the words: "These are the Olympics. You die for them." Then he threw a Games record to take gold.

Oerter was the first track and field athlete to win the same event in four successive Olympics, a feat equalled only once, by long jumper Carl Lewis in 1996. Each time, Oerter defeated the world record holder at the time and set an Olympic record. "In 1956, I beat inexperience; in 1960, public expectation; in 1964, injury; and then in 1968, I beat old age," he said.

Oerter went to the Melbourne Games aged only 20 and upset the American world record holder Fortune Gordien by setting a personal best to claim the title.

In Rome in 1960 Oerter thanked his compatriot Rink Babka, who was in the lead until the fifth round and then sportingly told Oerter he was carrying his non-throwing arm too low as he rotated. Oerter adjusted his technique and threw another personal best to take the title. In 1962 he twice set world records. But before the 1964 Olympics he damaged his neck and then, while in Tokyo, slipped badly on a wet surface and tore cartilage in his ribs. Doctors advised six weeks' rest but the American insisted on having his ribs bandaged and then was given painkillers. After a series of disappointing throws, he put everything into his fifth attempt, which won him the title by 48cm.

In 1968 his compatriot Jay Silvester set an Olympic record in the qualifying round, though he and the other competitors seemed far more disturbed than Oerter when rain delayed the final. In the third round Oerter unleashed a throw of 64.78m, beating his personal best by nearly two metres.

By John Goodbody

Al Oerter competes in the discus event at the 1968 Olympics, which he went on to win, still wearing a neck brace because of his injury four years earlier.

British pair leap to glory

Men's and women's long jump | Athletics,

Tokyo, 1964

Britain had rarely been renowned for long jumping but all that changed in October 1964. First, Mary Rand broke the world record to become the first British woman to win Olympic athletics gold. Then, four days later, Lynn Davies upset the favourites in the men's final, becoming Britain's first male winner of an Olympic field event since 1908.

Rand headed the long jump qualifiers, as she had done four years earlier in Rome, and this time she was inspired in the final. Four of her jumps were personal bests, with her fifth, into a headwind, recorded at 6.76m. As she said afterwards: "I'm just so relieved that I'm not coming home a flop, and no one has to say, 'Hard luck, Mary, this time.'"

Davies had gone to the United States championships in June and finished fourth. It was won with 8.11m by Ralph Boston, the 1960 Olympic champion and world record holder. Davies said: "Boston and the Russian Igor Ter-Ovanesyan were my heroes. The target for Tokyo was to reach the final and maybe aim for a bronze medal."

Davies scraped through qualifying with 7.78m. "The conditions were the worst you can imagine. There was rain, gusts of wind and the cinder runway was cut up.

After Boston had his first jump, he came back to the shelter where the other competitors were sitting and said, 'No one is going to jump eight metres today'.

"Suddenly I thought I had the opportunity to win the thing because I had jumped more than eight metres in conditions like that in Cardiff. The Welsh gods must have been looking down on Tokyo. Had it been a warm sunny day I would not have won."

By the fifth round Davies was in third place behind Boston and Ter-Ovanesyan. "I waited until the wind dropped by looking at the flag at the top of the stadium. After it had dropped I took off. I knew it was a good jump."

Indeed it was, a Commonwealth record of 8.07m for first place. Davies said: "There was then just Boston between the gold medal and me. I couldn't watch and buried my head in my towel as he made his last effort. The officials took about two minutes to measure it. Slowly the numbers came up on the scoreboard, 8 and then 0 and then 3 – 8.03m." Davies was the champion.

By John Goodbody

Opposite Top – *Lynn Davies (left) greets fans with Ann Packer (centre), his British team-mate and fellow gold medallist, in 1964.*

Opposite Bottom – *Mary Rand displays her medals for photographers following her success at the 1964 games.*

Brave Věra enchants a nation

Women's gymnastics

Mexico City, 1968

The Czech gymnast Věra Čáslavská was initially a figure skater but switched to gymnastics when Eva Bosáková, then her country's premier exponent, asked girls to take part in a competition to unearth talent. "Perhaps there is a future world champion among you," Bosáková said.

Čáslavská was inspired, was chosen and started training twice a day. She gained a silver medal at the 1960 Olympics in the team event. Four years later Čáslavská won the all-around title. In April 1968 she signed the anti-communist protest manifesto 'Two Thousand Words' but four months later Soviet troops invaded her country. Čáslavská was in a training camp in Moravia and, having been told she might be arrested, hid from the authorities. She kept fit by lifting bags of coal, swinging from trees and practising her floor routine in a field.

She was eventually allowed to join the rest of the Czech team. The gymnastics events were seen by the world as an opportunity for Čáslavská to show the spirit of her country was still alive. In winning four gold medals, including the all-around title, she produced an effervescent blend of beauty and technical excellence, never more so than in the floor exercises with her Mexican Hat Dance, which brought an ecstatic reception from the crowd.

By John Goodbody

Věra Čáslavská, of Czechoslovakia, performs on the vault during her gold medal-winning campaign at the 1968 Games in at Mexico City.

Peters puts Belfast troubles aside

Women's pentathlon | Athletics

Munich, 1972

From Neil Allen

Mary Peters, of Belfast, achieved the ultimate in an athlete's ambitions when she won a gold medal and set a world record at the end of the Olympic pentathlon. At 33, she scored 4,801 points after achieving personal records in four of the five events, spread over two days.

It was a glorious victory for someone who has been short both of training facilities and peace of mind, because she lives and works in a strife-torn city. As if glad to be released from the shadows into the harsh glitter of the Olympic arena, she proved to be the complete competitor.

After superb efforts in the 100 metres, shot putt and high jump, along with a commendable long jump, Miss Peters had the lead overall going into the final event, the 200 metres.

We calculated hastily that something close to 24 seconds could give Miss Peters the gold medal. When she kept driving her way in the heat in fourth place behind three Germans, unofficial times showed that she was close to her target.

Ahead of Miss Peters in that last race were her two biggest threats, Burglinde Pollak, of East Germany, who ran 22.96 seconds, and Heidemarie Rosendahl, of West Germany, with 23.93 seconds. There was a desperate five-minute wait. Miss Peters, her arm round the neck of Ann Wilson, her team-mate, stared at the electric scoreboard. Then up flashed the golden figures.

Mary Peters clears the high-jump bar at the 1972 Games, where she won gold for Britain.

America's monopoly ends in mayhem

Men's basketball

Munich, 1972

Few international sports events have ended in such confusion and controversy as the 1972 men's Olympic basketball final. The American team have never accepted their silver medals, believing they were robbed of the gold, though an inquiry by the International Olympic Committee upheld the Soviet Union's victory.

Basketball was admitted to the Olympic programme in 1936, when the United States began a run of 62 straight victories that lasted until that Munich final, using mainly college players. Nobody expected new champions in 1972 and the Americans reached the final with little trouble, though the score against Brazil was only 61-54.

The gold medal match began just before midnight in Munich for the convenience of US television viewers and, immediately, the favourites realised their invincible record was under threat. The Soviet team, with a strong representation from republics such as Lithuania and Latvia where basketball is particularly popular, led with 12 minutes left when Dwight Jones, the USA's top scorer, and the Soviet reserve Ivan Edeshko were ejected from the game after a loose-ball scuffle.

That should have hindered the Americans, but they began to reduce the deficit and, with 10 seconds left, Alexsandr Belov blundered by throwing the ball to the American Doug Collins, who charged up the court. He was fouled attempting a lay-up and was awarded two free throws. The crowd watched in fascinated silence as the groggy Collins sank both of them to put the United States ahead 50-49. Three seconds remained.

The Soviet team had no time to reply but, as the Americans began celebrating, the head referee, Renato Righetto, spotted gesturing at the scorers' table. He went over and learnt that the Soviet coach had called a time-out, as he was entitled to do, after Collins's first shot. The horn had sounded after the first basket by Collins but in the excitement the officials had not halted play. A further second was allowed and again the Soviet Union could do nothing in the time. Once more the Americans celebrated.

Then William Jones, the British secretary-general of the International Basketball Federation (FIBA), intervened, although strictly speaking he was not entitled to do so. Jones declared that the clock be set back three seconds to match the moment the time-out had been called. This time a long pass was hurled to Belov, who swept past two defenders to score and make the result 51-50.

Soviet supporters and officials raced on to the court to form a huge pile of bodies, under which were the joyous team. The Americans promptly protested that the extra three seconds should not have been allowed. FIBA convened a jury of appeal and this divided along the political lines of the Cold War.

The Polish and Cuban members voted that the result should stand, while those from Puerto Rico and Italy stated the basket of Belov should not count. The chairman was Hungarian and he cast the decisive opinion for the Soviet Union to be awarded the gold medal.

By John Goodbody

The US and Soviet teams compete for the ball at the tip off in the 1972 men's basketball final.

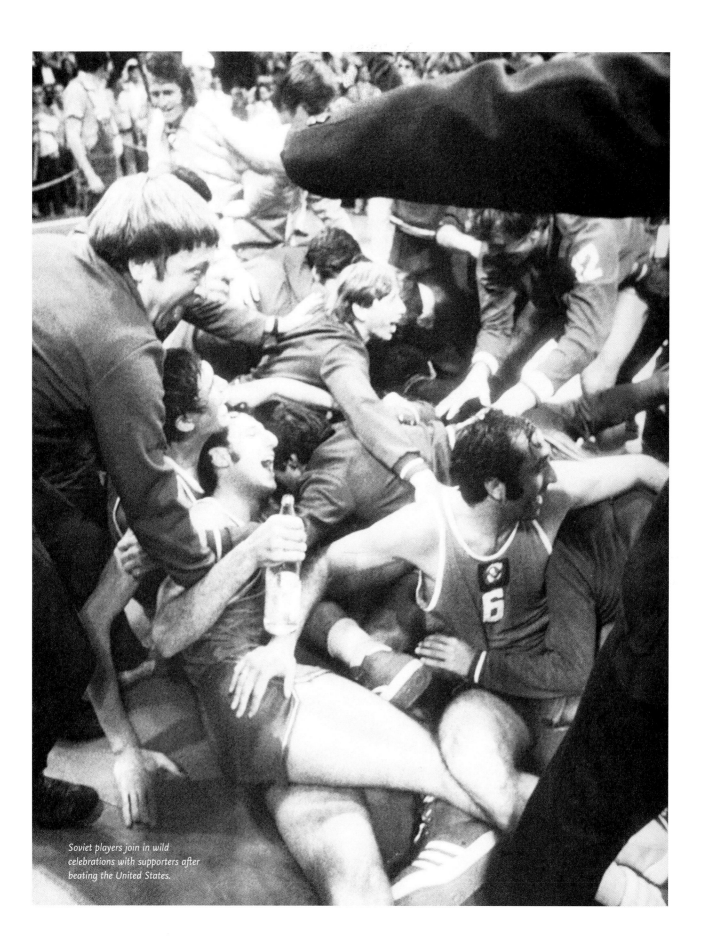

Soviet players join in wild celebrations with supporters after beating the United States.

Soviet basketball player Ivan Edeshko celebrates after his side's controversial victory over the United States.

Yamashita hobbles to heroic success

Men's open category | Judo

Los Angeles, 1984

FROM NICHOLAS SOAMES

Yasuhiro Yamashita, the greatest judo champion of all time, drew the cloak of invincibility closer around his shoulders when, in a fitting finale to the Olympic judo competition, he won the open category with an unparalleled display of ability and character.

In his second bout, against the West German, Arthur Schnabel, he severely pulled a calf muscle when attempting to throw and to all intents and purposes, he fought his two remaining contests on one leg and a prop. In fact, he had to be helped on to the victory rostrum by the silver medal winner, the Egyptian, Mohamed Rashwan.

Not one of his four opponents approached the technical standard of Yamashita who, at 27, is unbeaten since 1977. In round three, the current European Open champion, a Frenchman, Laurent del Colombo, showing no mercy, attacked determinedly and threw the champion for a knockdown score – the first time the Japanese champion had been scored against since 1977.

For his temerity, Del Colombo was 10 seconds later catapulted backwards by a hooking throw and held down by Yamashita. And even on one leg Yamashita's final against Rashwan, who is no mean fighter, was a mere formality. In victory, the conqueror broke into tears. And even at this stage he revealed a basic humility.

"If I had been a great Olympic champion I would not have injured myself while winning," Yamashita was heard to say.

Japan's Yasuhiro Yamashita (centre) celebrates winning gold at Los Angeles 1984 despite suffering a bad leg injury early in the competition. Mihai Cioc (left), of Romania, won bronze while the Egyptian Mohamed Ali Rashwan (right) took silver.

Louganis goes from disaster to delight

Men's three-metre springboard | Diving

Seoul, 1988

FROM STEVEN DOWNES

The crowd that filled the Jamsil pool in Seoul yesterday for the final of the men's springboard were there to see whether the world's most celebrated diver, Greg Louganis, could recover from public humiliation.

In the preliminaries on Monday, the 27-year-old's head crashed against the board on his descent from a dive. Instead of his usual tally of scores, he was awarded a meagre total of just over six points.

Could he return the following day and defend his title, when all 12 finalists would restart on level terms? The answer was to be provided with his ninth-round dive. By that stage, he was already 20 points clear. What lay ahead was the dive which had beaten him the day before.

In fairness, a reverse two-and-a-half somersault in the pike position is one of the hardest. With most divers, the springboard event sounds like a storm in reverse, the board's bend providing the thunder, the diver's entry giving the lightning crash. Yet with Louganis, there is an odd silence after he leaves the board, as he whispers through his manoeuvres high in the air, and then enters the water perfectly, hardly creating a ripple.

So it was on this occasion. The relief showed as Louganis lifted himself on to the poolside. Despite the stitches on the crown of his head causing him pain whenever he smiled, he was beaming. He had done more than just win an Olympic gold medal.

Above – Greg Louganis, of the United States, rubs his head after hitting the springboard in the preliminary rounds at Seoul 1988. Louganis recovered from the accident to win gold.

Opposite – Louganis hits his head on the springboard.

Redmond wins hearts with his dad

Men's 400 metres | Athletics

Barcelona, 1992

Most athletes are recalled for the races they won. Derek Redmond is remembered for the race he finished. Despite tearing a hamstring, the British 400 metres runner hobbled round the Barcelona track in tears – supported by his father, who had rushed down from the stands – to become one of the most indelible Olympic images.

The events of that 1992 semi-final are popular on YouTube, with almost two million hits on the sequence used by the International Olympic Committee in its Celebrate Humanity series. Decades later, Redmond still received emails nearly every day from viewers.

He was the British record-holder whose individual career was blighted by injury. Fate repeatedly dealt him a bad hand. He missed the 1986 Commonwealth and 1988 Olympic Games and was rarely in his best form at big events, although he won relay gold at the Commonwealth Games and European championships and at the 1991 world championships.

Then came 1992. "I had had some injury problems as usual but I scrambled through. I arrived in Spain about three weeks before the Games and had my best two weeks of training leading up to the first round. I was pretty much flying. I ran my fastest ever time trial for 300 metres and in the first round I was aiming at about 45.5 seconds."

Instead he ran 45 seconds. "I couldn't believe it was that fast. It had seemed like a walk in the park." Redmond did 45.1s in the next round, again coasting home. He was not planning to run the semi-final any faster but was quickly away and making up the stagger when he heard a pop and stopped at 150m, clutching the back of his right leg. He slumped down, his hands on the track. "Then I thought, 'This is the Olympic semi-final. I will see if I can catch them.'"

So he rose and began hopping. At 200m he looked for the rest of the runners. "They had finished and had probably disappeared down the tunnel. Then I thought it might be my last race, so I decided I was going to get to the end."

A few officials tried to stop him but he kept going and then suddenly his father, Jim, was at his side. Distraught at his son's plight, he had come down from the stand, evading officials. He told Derek: "You don't have to do this, son." "Yes, I do," Derek replied. "Then we will finish it together."

By John Goodbody

Britain's Derek Redmond is helped to the finish line by his father, Jim, after tearing a hamstring during a semi-final of the 400 metres at Barcelona 1992.

Courageous Strug defies injury

Women's team event | Gymnastics

Atlanta, 1996

FROM ANDREW LONGMORE

When these Games are over, Atlanta should erect a statue to Kerri Strug. It would not need to be very big. Lifesize would be a mere 4ft 9in tall. Because the American gymnast has produced a sporting story of courage and sacrifice translatable into every language in the world.

Her moment came in the team competition, with the US team at risk of losing to Russia. The 18-year-old had injured her left ankle so badly in her first attempt at the vault that it was now heavily strapped. The Americans, however, needed her to score strongly to secure gold.

Standing on the runway, with her ankle throbbing, Strug had to make a choice. She could have limped away, claimed the sympathy vote and protected herself for the all-around event, the blue riband of gymnastics. Instead, urged on by her coach, the ebullient Béla Károlyi, she ignored the pain and lifted her muscular little frame for one final effort.

She landed, momentarily, on both feet before hopping on to her right one to salute the judges. Her score of 9.712 was enough to win.

"I have had to deal with so much pain before," Strug said. "I thought I could deal with one last vault. I said a little prayer before I went: 'Please God, help me out. I've done this vault a thousand times. Let me do it one more time.'"

Left – Kerri Strug feels her injured ankle at the 1996 Games. Despite the injury, she helped the United States win gold in the team vault competition.

Opposite – Strug lands her vault on an injured ankle to help the United States win gymnastics gold.

Freeman unites a nation

Women's 400 metres | Athletics

Sydney, 2000

FROM OLIVER HOLT

She used the last of her strength to pull back the hood of the bodysuit that she says makes her feel special and sat down hard on the track. It seemed then that all we could see was her noble face. Somehow, flooding into its gasping, heaving contours, all the hopes and dreams of a more compassionate Australia were coming together. A nation was shedding its guilt and voicing its hope for a better future in the face of Cathy Freeman.

Freeman was not just running for herself when she burst out of the blocks at the start of the women's 400 metres in the Olympic Stadium last night. She was not even running just for her nation. She was running for Australia and for Aboriginal communities, a state and a people who have been in conflict for too long.

"The race of all our lives," one newspaper had called it yesterday morning because it knew reconciliation was at hand. It felt like the race of all our lives here in the stadium, too. From the crack of the starter's gun and the roar that accompanied it, it felt that there was a force running with her. It felt somehow that goodness was on her side, that emotion simply could not let her lose. If ever a collective will has urged an athlete to win a race, it was here last night.

The people carried her, just as she has carried them. Perhaps it should not have mattered that she won. But when this woman, whose grandfather had been prevented from pursuing a sporting career because of restrictions on freedom of movement, stood on the top step of the podium and sang the words "Advance Australia Fair" at the top of her voice, it felt as though a corner had been turned in the life of this nation.

"When I crossed the line I just felt relief," Freeman said. "I was totally overwhelmed because I could feel the crowd around me and all over me. I felt everybody's emotions and their happiness and their joy. It was pouring into every corner of my body. I just had to sit down and get comfortable. The whole thing was beyond words.

"What has happened tonight, what I symbolise, will make a difference to the attitude of a lot of people – people in politics, people in sport, ordinary people in Australia," she said. "I've made a lot of people happy tonight, a lot of people from different backgrounds and I am happy myself about that. My coach kept telling me I was going to win, but I didn't want to believe him."

If there is anger inside her about the way Aboriginal peoples were persecuted, about the generations of her people that were stolen away from their communities, she does not show it. Last night, when she had recovered her composure after the race, she walked slowly to the crowd and grasped an Australian flag and an Aboriginal flag that had been tied together and danced her lap of honour with them draped over her shoulders. "I don't think things really get much better than this," Freeman said.

Australia's Cathy Freeman crosses the finish line to win gold in the 400 metres at Sydney. Behind her, Mexico's Ana Guevara finishes fifth.

Kelly Holmes rounds the pack to take the lead during the 1,500 metres in Athens.

Holmes lands golden double

Women's 1,500 metres | Athletics

Athens, 2004

FROM ROB HUGHES, FOR *THE SUNDAY TIMES*

At 8.33pm in the Olympic stadium of Athens last night, Kelly Holmes went into overdrive. She came round the outside of an entire field of middle-distance runners, her pace akin to a Ferrari coming out of the slipstream of seemingly one sedate Ford after another. And we, the Brits starved of any other individual gold medallist in the track and field squad we sent out to these Games, were shocked by the form, the power, the certainty of it all.

Holmes, 20 years a runner, three times an Olympian, and now arguably the class athlete of these Games on their return to the place of their origin. We look at her. The body that has let her down in numerous stadiums now so thoroughly honed, so powerful and so enduring: small wonder that her first words after the triumph were to thank Alison Rose, the Sheffield physiotherapist who over the past two months had treated her body, but also listened to her mental anguish. "Ali was on the phone for me day after day. She's helped to keep me in one piece, and I've told Ali more than I told anybody else about what's inside me."

Consider what Holmes has achieved in the past nine days. When she knelt on the track after the finish of the 1,500 metres, her head cradled in her hands, her body throbbing with emotion and possibly fatigue, she was the only British athlete to win a gold medal on the track at these Games. An hour later, the men's 4 x 100 metres relay team, surely inspired by her, delivered. But Holmes, draped in two Union flags, one for each of her triumphs, was the first British

Holmes is jubilant as she wins the 1,500 metres.

female ever to win two track titles at one Olympics. She equalled two of the most renowned middle-distance runners in history, Svetlana Masterkova in 1996 and Tatyana Kazankina in 1976, who had pulled off this double.

Holmes said: "I keep thinking somebody is going to come and wake me up – that it's a dream and I still have the final to run."

Having spent almost three hours with her on the eve of this Olympiad, I know how she yearned to win a medal. Not necessarily a gold, she said, but a medal to prove to her what passion and years of hard work could achieve.

She was talking as a "clean" athlete, before a Games that was to expose more contaminated drug cheats than any other. Yet when she cruised around the finalists yesterday, there was an eerie lack of camaraderie, an initial lack of human response to her. It was a little shocking. Later, Tatyana Tomashova, the Russian silver medallist, said that she had relied on her sprint, but with Holmes it was good enough only for second place. Maria Cioncan, the Romanian who won bronze, admitted: "I tried to stay behind Kelly Holmes for as long as possible, but I couldn't follow her pace." Nobody at these Olympics could.

HEROES

Pietri denied gold despite marathon effort

Men's marathon | Athletics

London, 1908

FROM A *TIMES* REPORTER

Johnny Hayes (USA) was awarded first place in the marathon race yesterday. Dorando Pietri (Italy) struggled home first, but a protest was raised against him for being assisted round the track in the stadium, and he was disqualified.

Pietri gave a most wonderful exhibition of pluck and endurance. When he entered the White City Stadium he was practically in a state of collapse, and late last night a report was circulated that he was dead. Happily, this proved to be incorrect, and the latest information received was that he had been able to leave for his home in Soho. Pietri is an Italian by birth and 22 years of age.

At the dinner given last night by his Majesty's Government to the Olympic council, Lord Desborough announced that the Queen would present a cup to Pietri as a mark of recognition of his splendid performance.

A glorious hot July afternoon, with hardly a breath of wind, was ideal for a bathe or a game of cricket perhaps, but terrible for a feat of endurance.

When Pietri burst into the White City Stadium in the lead, he looked dazed, bewildered, hardly conscious, in red shorts and white vest, his hair white with dust, staggering on to the track.

He looked about him, hardly knowing where he was. By some desperate resolve of determination, he needed to get round 200 yards to the tape of the finish. After 50 yards, he fell on the track, got up, staggered on a few yards and fell again, and yet again; and then reached the last turn.

By now, he was surrounded by officials almost, if not quite, supporting him, urging him on. He could not run straight. There was almost a horrible parody of a spurt. He dropped again ten yards from the tape, rose, staggered forward over those last terrible few yards, and reached the goal.

Hayes had followed him into the stadium, a long way behind him in time, but comparatively a fresh and strong man. He could not quite catch Pietri up, though he had run a magnificent race.

The Americans protested against Pietri's win on the ground that he received assistance, and the protest was finally sustained.

Altogether the finish of the race was far from satisfactory. The rule about attendants not being allowed on the course was flagrantly broken. But it seemed inhuman to leave Pietri to struggle on unaided, and inhuman to urge him to continue.

And yet, the race was not to the stadium entrance, but to the finish in front of the Royal box, and it is extremely doubtful whether, by his own unaided exertions, Pietri could ever have got so far. And the Americans are entitled to claim the actual winner.

An exhausted Dorando Pietri breaks the tape in the 1908 Olympics marathon in London. The Italian was stripped of gold because he was helped across the finish line by officials.

Elliott wins by a country mile

Men's 1,500 metres | Athletics

Rome, 1960

Herb Elliott, the brilliant Australian, broke his own world record in winning the 1,500 metres by an astonishing 18m in Rome's Olympic Stadium. Even for Elliott, it was a remarkable performance and prompted Michel Jazy, the silver medallist, to describe his opponent as "like a being from another planet".

With the field having been strung out by an already exhausting pace, Elliott increased the pressure on his opponents 600m from the finish, which put him clearly ahead on the bell.

As he reached the final stretch, Elliott's coach Percy Cerutty leapt over the moat surrounding the track, tore off his white shirt and waved it to indicate Elliott was on course to break his world record. It was a pre-arranged signal between the two men, although Elliott had forgotten the meaning of it. However, as the police hauled away Cerutty, Elliott's failure to understand his coach did not matter as he ran 3min 35.6s, beating his previous landmark by 0.4s.

A regime of pounding up sand dunes, lifting heavy weights and eating masses of rolled oats and fresh fruit had served Elliott well and he remained unbeaten over 1,500 metres and the mile for the rest of his career.

By Robert Dineen

Australia's Herb Elliott wins the 1,500 metres at Rome 1960, beating the field by 18 metres to break his own world record with a time of 3 minutes 35.6 seconds.

Snell stuns field with electric finish

Men's 1,500 metres | Athletics

Tokyo, 1964

FROM OUR OLYMPICS CORRESPONDENT

Peter Snell, the New Zealand athlete, produced a devastating kick to add the 1,500 metres title to the 800 metres he won last week.

Snell almost toyed with the 1,500 metres field and then unleashed a final 400m in 53.2s, which is the fastest finish he had ever shown. Frenchman Michel Bernard, John Whetton and John Davies, both of Great Britain, were the pace-setters, but when the burly Snell decided to take over there was no reply.

Snell, 25, owes a debt of gratitude to Arthur Lydiard, New Zealand's renowned athletics coach, who has worked with Snell since he was aged 19.

Lydiard has Snell regularly running 22 miles in sessions, something that previously was not commonplace for 800 metres and 1,500 metres specialists. Four years ago, the preparation helped him to win the 800 metres in Rome. In the same event at these Games, he broke away from the field with 200m left to win in 1min 45.1s. By also winning the 1,500 metres he has become the first athlete to win the Olympic middle-distance double since Britain's Albert Hill in 1920.

Peter Snell takes the lead in the men's 1,500 metres final in 1964.

Dutch ace humbles Japan

Men's open category | Judo

Tokyo, 1964

FROM OUR OLYMPIC GAMES STAFF

Physically dominant and technically precise, Anton Geesink has become the first foreigner to beat the Japanese in the sport they invented, winning the Olympic title in Tokyo, where judo has been included at the Games for the first time.

Although 1.98m and more than 120kg, the Dutchman did not rely on his size and strength, preferring to use skill, particularly with swift ankle throws executed with timing rather than force.

Home fighters have won the three weight classes but the prize they craved was the open (unlimited weight) title, in which they fielded the 105kg Akio Kaminaga, three times All-Japan champion.

In a preliminary pool the Dutchman defeated Kaminaga but the Japanese athlete won his remaining contests and faced Geesink in the final. For the first time in the tournament the Emperor was not present. He clearly feared what would happen.

After nearly nine minutes of the contest, Kaminaga attacked and Geesink countered, grabbing a leg as the pair fell to the mat. Geesink finally secured a hold-down as the Japanese athlete desperately squirmed underneath him. When the necessary 30 seconds ran down to seal Geesink's win, the elderly masters of the sport looked on impassively. Japanese team members were in tears at the side of the mat.

Anton Geesink of the Netherlands holds down Japan's Akio Kaminaga during the Judo final at the 1964 Olympics.

Ice-cool Viren leaves rivals trailing

Men's 5,000 metres | Athletics

Montreal, 1976

FROM NEIL ALLEN

Lasse Virén, of Finland, became the first man in the history of the Olympics to retain both the 5,000 and 10,000 metres titles when he won the 5,000 metres this evening, in 13min 24.76s against the highest quality opposition, with a consummate demonstration of self-control and self-confidence.

Fine runners, in their time, like Dick Quax and Rodney Dixon, of New Zealand, and Brendan Foster, of Britain, were left languishing as Viren strode away in the final home straight, completing his final lap in 55.1s as coolly as if he had just been for a dip in one of those chilly Finnish lakes.

Behind him Quax took the silver and Klaus-Peter Hildenbrand of West Germany, falling on his right side, but with all of his body down to his thighs safely over the line, was third, just in front of Dixon.

There was, of course, only one man really in this race and that was the Finn who, in the heat of the moment, I would almost bracket with the great Paavo Nurmi as a distance racer. He ran with the complete command that Jack Lovelock, of New Zealand, showed in the 1936 Olympic 1,500 metres, always knowing what he was doing, erect, poised, while about him the others were almost struck with stage-fright by the aloof, unshakable presence of their master.

After Foster had set the pace for the first 800 metres, Viren waited until there were seven laps to go before taking his place at the head of the queue. He stayed there for two more laps, let Foster accelerate briefly, and then Hildenbrand take over.

With just two laps left to run the order was Viren, Foster, Quax, Britain's Ian Stewart and Hildenbrand, as the Russian, Boris Kuznetsov, took one of the tumbles which have been so characteristic of the racing here.

What was memorable, as the medal seekers came chasing down the last straight, was the moment when Quax twice turned to his left and looked at the fleeing figure of Viren striding away so majestically from him. Quax must have known in his heart then that the man was unbeatable.

Finland's Lasse Viren wins the 5,000 metres at Montreal 1976 ahead of Dick Quax (left) of New Zealand, and West Germany's Klaus-Peter Hildenbrand (right), who collapsed to the ground after claiming bronze.

Stevenson reigns supreme

Men's super-heavyweight | Boxing

Moscow, 1980

FROM A SUNDAY TIMES CORRESPONDENT

Teofilo Stevenson extended his dominance over the super-heavyweight division of Olympic boxing by winning his third consecutive gold medal in Moscow. The Cuban had pledged his solidarity with his socialist hosts, but his defeat over the Soviet fighter Pyotr Zayev in the final still drew whistles of derision from the home crowd.

It was not Stevenson's smoothest performance against an opponent who gave away six inches and two stone to the champion. Zayev withstood the Cuban's usually devastating right hand and was likely grateful that Stevenson chose not to attack his stomach, instead jabbing away in an ultimately unsuccessful effort to bring down his guard.

By the final round, Zayev wore a small, boyish smile, as if proud in the knowledge that Stevenson was not going to hurt him. But the challenger also did not get close to hurting the champion.

According to the Cuban News Agency, Stevenson has won 188 of his 201 fights, the overwhelming percentage of them by knockout. He has now gone three Olympics unbeaten. With no prospect of him turning professional, it would appear there is little left for him to conquer, aged just 28.

Teofilo Stevenson in action during the heavyweight competition at the 1980 Games in Moscow, where the Cuban won gold for the third consecutive Olympics.

Moses scales the heights

Men's 400 metres hurdles | Athletics

Los Angeles, 1984

FROM OUR CORRESPONDENT

Ed Moses added a second gold medal in the 400 metres hurdles to the one he won eight years ago with a devastating performance in the final in Los Angeles. The American athlete who has said he wanted to be known as "the guy nobody could beat" has now gone seven years unbeaten.

With Moses having set a new world record earlier this month, the 28-year-old's triumph here was widely expected. Only the West German Harald Schmidt was thought likely to provide competition, although he ended up third, with Danny Harris, the teenage American, taking silver. He finished in 48.13s, while Moses, with his famous three-metre stride, triumphed in 47.75s – quick, but short of his 47.13s world record.

Moses was denied a shot at the 1980 title because of the United States boycott of the Moscow Games, but his legacy is secured. The American team coach LeRoy Walker said: "Extraordinary talent is obvious. We're in the rarefied presence of an immortal here. Edwin's a crowd unto himself."

Away from the track, Moses has been heavily involved in ensuring athletes can legitimately claim adequate compensation for training expenses and money from sponsorship and competing without jeopardising Olympic participation. The Games should be grateful to be able to showcase a talent of his calibre as a result.

Above – Ed Moses on the track after winning the 400 metres hurdles at the 1984 Games.

Opposite – Moses celebrates extending his seven-year unbeaten run in the event.

Elvstrom bows out in style

Tornado | Sailing

Seoul, 1988

FROM OUR CORRESPONDENT IN BUSAN, SOUTH KOREA

Not many Olympians who finish 15th are applauded by their peers but Paul Elvstrøm is unique. The Danish sailor, who competed here with his daughter Trine in the Tornado class, won Olympic golds in 1948, 1952, 1956 and 1960. For the sailors gathered to shake his hand in Busan, it was a privilege just to be in the same regatta as Elvstrøm, the 60-year-old widely regarded as the finest small boats exponent in history.

Brought up near the sea, Elvstrøm began racing at nine, though his teenage activity was disturbed by the war. Aged 20, he was picked for the single-handed class in 1948, and squeezed into the lead on the final day for victory.

Elvstrøm used toe straps to a greater extent than had been done before and exercised by hanging off a boat simulator in his garage. He also tried to sail every day, whatever the weather, to train his reactions. The hard work was rewarded in the Finn class in 1952 when he won Olympic gold with a race to spare. He was victorious in Melbourne and, four years later in the Bay of Naples, he was assured of the gold medal before the final day's racing. Twelve years after his fourth Olympic victory, he suffered a nervous breakdown and took a break from the sport.

He returned intermittently, including at the Los Angeles Games where Elvstrøm and Trine became the first father and daughter to compete at the Olympics. He was disappointed only to win bronze.

A dyslexic who set out to prove himself in sport, Elvstrøm's competitive instinct has never left him. "As I get older, I like faster and faster boats," he says, adding: "Winning is not the only thing, but it is the most fun, that's for sure."

He might not have won a medal here, but he will be remembered as a champion.

Danish sailor Paul Elvstrøm with his daughter Trine in the tornado event at the 1984 Games in Los Angeles. They were the first father and daughter to compete together at an Olympics.

'Zip' celebrates climbing to the top

Women's athletics

Barcelona Paralympics, 1992

The extraordinary career of Zipora Rubin-Rosenbaum was finally over. The versatile Israeli, at 46 years old, was competing in athletics, her seventh Paralympics, because she had such fond memories of the Games, and an event that had given her enormous satisfaction and made her a cherished figure in her home country.

She may have finished only eighth in the javelin and 13th in the shot as a wheelchair competitor, but her rivals saluted her for the legend that she is. And her drive for sporting excellence all began with a strawberry tree. Contracting polio at the age of four, she was forced to walk with the aid of a frame but refused to give up. If other girls performed a handstand, then Zip, as she is known to her friends, also wanted to do a handstand.

The strawberry tree near her home was particularly significant. She was often ignored at school, saying she was "treated like a rag" and when all the other girls could climb the tree, she was determined to do the same herself. "Every day I would go there. I kept going and, in the end, I succeeded," she said.

In 1964, she competed in her first Paralympics taking three medals in athletics, including gold and a world record in the shot, and other medals in swimming and table tennis. That was just the beginning. Over 28 years she won a total of 30 medals.

By John Goodbody

Zipora Rubin-Rosenbaum at the 1966
International Stoke Mandeville Games, which later
became the Paralympics.

Edgson enters Paralympic folklore

Men's swimming

Barcelona Paralympics, 1992

By John Goodbody

The Paralympics have ended with Canadian Michael Edgson, whose achievements in Barcelona followed his triumphs in the two previous Games, having entered the folklore of para sport. Across the range of disciplines, especially the individual medley – the hallmark of the all-round swimmer – Edgson, 33, has impressed observers with his stamina and technical talent.

Dr Peter Vizsolyi, his coach at the University of Victoria, has said that one of Michael's characteristics was his determination to compete to the level of non-disabled swimmers. This has been the focus since Michael's sight was damaged as a child living in North Vancouver, when medication, prescribed for an illness, damaged his optic nerve. Michael took up the sport, aged 11, after trying several other activities including gymnastics, ice-hockey and football.

His most notable victories in Spain have been in the 200 metre and 400 metre individual medley.

Although initially concentrating on freestyle in the 1984 Games, he has added a proficiency in both backstroke and butterfly, which were especially evident in these Paralympic events.

Michael once met ice-hockey legend Wayne Gretzky who told him: "Those who are truly great need not talk about it." In his home, Michael does not even display his medals, keeping just two of them in a drawer.

The closing ceremony for the 1992 Paralympic Games in Barcelona.

Johnson has the world at his feet

Men's 200 metres | Athletics

Atlanta, 1996

From David Powell, Athletics Correspondent

Michael Johnson went to Planet Hollywood on Thursday night, but which planet had he come from? The world record which Johnson set in the 200 metres here was the most extraordinary Olympic performance since Bob Beamon skipped 28 feet at the 1968 Mexico Games, taking the long jump mark straight from 27ft to 29ft. Arguably, it was more extraordinary because Beamon enjoyed the benefit of altitude. Johnson was superhuman.

Yesterday, as Atlanta tried to concentrate on the penultimate day of competition on the track, nothing could deflect one's thinking from what had gone on the night before. Johnson had achieved the first Olympic 200/400 metres double by a man, but this historic achievement was lost in the disbelief that this Texan had run 19.32s for 200 metres.

Johnson covered the first 100 metres in 10.12s, on a curve. He ran the second 100 metres in 9.20s, albeit with a rolling start. His two 100-metre runs average out at 9.66s. Johnson cut the biggest slice off the world record since Eddie Tolan's 21.12s at the Los Angeles Games of 1932. Both Johnson and Tolan, also from the United States, improved it by 0.34s.

Tolan's record stood for 20 years. Johnson's will probably last beyond the lifetime of everybody who saw it. "I want to give people something to remember," he had said coming into the Games. He gave us more than we thought humanly possible.

Until June, when Johnson ran 19.66s in the US Olympic trials, the world record, held by Pietro Mennea, from Italy, had stood for 17 years. How long will it be before the combination of forces which

Michael Johnson, of the United States, celebrates winning the 200 metres in a world record time of 19.32 seconds at the 1996 Games.

brought Johnson to this pinnacle meet again? A fast track, a capacity home crowd of 83,000, a warm evening ideal for sprinting, favourable wind, and the incentive of the double to drive on a magnificent athlete at his peak.

Given that the track is to be pulled up after the Paralympics which follow these Games, and Johnson is unlikely to be inspired to this degree again, it is hard to imagine even the great man himself going quicker. Johnson, after two frustrating Olympic campaigns, won here by the biggest margin since Jesse Owens in 1936.

Of his second 100 metres, run at an average speed of 24.45 miles per hour, Johnson remarked: "It really blows me away." Certainly it blew the opposition away. Though leading by barely the length of one of his 3.5oz gold-laminated spikes coming off the bend, Johnson's acceleration was so sudden it was as though the other seven finalists had a conveyor belt beneath their feet, moving towards them.

Hart was asked about the physiological testing his athlete had undergone. "The only thing I know," Hart replied, "is that, when they took off his shirt, there was a big S on his chest." It must have been the Daily Planet he came from.

Johnson leads down the home straight
in the 400 metres in Atlanta.

Brutal 'bouncer' is beaten at last

Men's 130kg | Greco-Roman wrestling

Sydney, 2000

FROM JOHN GOODBODY

Americans call Aleksandr Karelin "The Bouncer in the Meanest Bar in Hell". Few sportsmen have been as intimidating as the Russia's Greco-Roman wrestling champion, but time finally caught up with him in Sydney as a 13-year unbeaten run came to an end in the superheavyweight final.

Aged 33, and having suffered a series of injuries, Karelin was beaten by Rulon Gardner, from Wyoming. Karelin slipped behind early on when he was penalised for briefly releasing his grip around his rival's body. Gardner then fought a defensive contest to protect his narrow lead and, for once, Karelin could not make up the difference.

The victory meant Gardner exacted some revenge on Karelin. During his defeat by the Russian at the 1997 world championships, Gardner had been subject to Karelin's signature move, a reverse body lift. It involves him placing his hands underneath his rival's stomach, throwing him backwards before landing on top of him. "I'd never flown before," Gardner said at the time. "It was cool."

With his scarred, shaven head, large ears and hooded eyelids, as well as a 6ft 4in frame and a weight of nearly 21st, Karelin has cut a frightening figure during his reign over the sport. It comes to an end with a formidable list of achievements, including three Olympic, nine world and 12 European titles.

Aleksandr Karelin (left), tangles with Rulon Gardner, of the United States, in the gold-medal bout during the Greco-Roman wrestling competition at the 2000 Olympics. The American prevented his Russian opponent from winning gold at a fourth successive Games.

Fu seizes chance for immortality

Women's three-metre springboard | Diving

Sydney, 2000

From Simon Barnes, Chief Sports Writer

She's Steve Redgrave's soul sister. She's 5ft 3in and 7st 10lb, and only 21, but Redgrave would recognise the mind. Pure diamond. It's the hardness I am thinking of, not the sparkle. Fu Mingxia. You'll be familiar with her, if not by name. Eight years ago, she was the little waif of Barcelona. The 13-year-old who won gold in those Games, showing a sternness older than her years and an innocence rather younger. She went to the Atlanta Olympics four years older and a couple of stone heavier. Now she could make that springboard ping. And she won her second Olympic gold on the platform that year, and then picked up her third in the springboard.

She is, of course, a product of the troubling Chinese hothouse system: taken away from her parents, subjected to long and hard discipline. And unsurprisingly, after Atlanta and discovering a mind of her own, she walked away from it all. She had brought her state enough glory, after all. She went to Tsinghua University in Beijing and studied economics. Grew out her standard issue Chinese bob. Did things like listen to pop music. For the first time in her life, she was young.

And she found she didn't want to give it up after all. "I still think diving is very charming," she said. "I like it very much, that's why I came back." She was not selected for the platform this time, but she won silver as half of a pair in the women's synchronised diving, a new sport at these Games. But she was on a quest that required a gold medal. Were she to win one, she would equal the women's record of Pat McCormick, who won four diving gold medals, two each at the 1952 and 1956 Olympics.

Fu came into the diving finals last night in second place after the semi-finals, behind her compatriot, Guo Jingjing. Guo fell short in the fourth dive and for the first time Fu was in the lead. Guo made her final dive knowing that she needed something close to perfection and the wish got in the way of the deed. Fu still needed a very good dive and she won it like a champion: a reverse one and half somersaults piked with two and a half twists. She absolutely ripped the entry and emerged from the water the greatest female diver the world has ever seen. "I don't regard myself as special," she said afterwards. "I am the equal of all the others in the team."

China's Fu Mingxia competes in the women's three-metre springboard event at Atlanta 1996 on her way to her second gold medal of the games, and third in total.

Thorpe triumphs with power and poise

Men's 200 metres freestyle | Swimming

Athens, 2004

FROM SIMON BARNES, CHIEF SPORTS WRITER

Ian Thorpe, the only man on earth with gills, won the race that was seen as the greatest head-to-head at this Olympic Games, and he did it as a champion should.

It was a performance that held power and serenity in the most extraordinary state of balance. Hard to find such qualities co-existing in any walk of life, the last place you expect to witness these things in such perfect harmony is in the Olympic swimming pool. Last night, Thorpe, of Australia, won the 200 metres freestyle in an Olympic record time of 1min 44.71s and did so with the languid grace you normally see in a shark.

This was the showdown between Thorpe and Michael Phelps, of the United States. The entire men's swimming meet is something of a private duel between the two of them; the score in gold medals is now 2-1 in Thorpe's favour. Phelps could manage only a bronze last night, always looking laboured alongside the impossible smoothness of the Thorpe stroke.

At one stage, Pieter van den Hoogenband, who finished with silver, looked as if he might throw everyone's calculations out with a storming start, leading through the first two lengths in a world record schedule. But coming back again up the pool, you could see the balance of the race change decisively.

The Dutchman seemed to slow up. Mind you, so did Thorpe. But that's what Thorpe does; he creates the strange and captivating illusion of moving more and more slowly as he reaches for his greatest effort. Everyone else looks as if he is doing the hardest work he has done his life. Everyone else looks as if he is giving his all. But the bizarre truth of the matter is that only Thorpe is actually doing so. No one else has the supreme hydrodynamic efficiency; no one else has the perfect piscine ability to translate movement in the water into speed. And down that final length, everyone else went into furious, foaming overdrive while Thorpe reached out a benign hand to caress the water away. Everyone else has to fight the water; Thorpe co-operates with it. And behind him those famous size 17 feet whipped the water into Guinness.

In victory, the illusion – or the reality – of serenity was abruptly discarded, the yellow cap ripped from his head, the seal's pelt of hair exposed and a great air-punching, lung-ripping primeval roar of triumph. The fish in him could now be set aside to allow the triumph of the human.

Australia's Ian Thorpe celebrates winning the 200 metres freestyle at the 2004 Games in Athens.

El Guerrouj banishes his Olympic jinx

Men's 1,500 metres | Athletics

Athens, 2004

FROM DAVID POWELL

At twenty to midnight here last night, Hicham El Guerrouj won the 1,500 metres gold medal that his contribution to athletics craved, emerging triumphant from an epic race.

In the past eight years, before last night, the Moroccan had lost only five races out of 89 at 1,500 metres or the mile. But two had been in Olympic finals and two were on the grand prix circuit this year.

The auguries were not good. In 1996, at the Atlanta Games, he fell and, at Sydney 2000, he was beaten into second place by Noah Ngeny, from Kenya. In his last race before coming here, El Guerrouj was edged out by Bernard Lagat from Kenya, in Zurich.

Lagat had his own reasons for needing the victory. He had missed the World Championships last year while facing a two-year ban for testing positive for EPO. The case was dropped after the analysis of the B sample did not corroborate the first finding.

Knowing that he had to run the finish out of his Kenyan opponent, El Guerrouj made his move 750 metres from home. Lagat stuck to him like a limpet and edged past 60 metres out. We sighed as the great man seemed caught in another Olympic tale of woe. How we underestimated him.

Whether Lagat weakened, or El Guerrouj quickened, it was hard to tell but the Moroccan reclaimed the lead and held his ground, winning in 3min 34.18s.

Hicham El Guerrouj, of Morocco, sinks to his knees after winning the 1,500 metres at Athens 2004. Kenya's Bernard Lagat, who finished second, and Rui Silva, the Portuguese bronze medallist, congratulate him.

Kayak queen puts rivals in shade

Women's K4 500 metres | Canoeing

Athens Paralympics, 2004

Birgit Fischer, the German canoeist, completed a historic double when she won the K4 final in Athens. As she lifted the paddle above her head in celebration, the 42-year-old became the first woman to win Olympic titles 24 years apart. Having won her first title aged only 18, she was also now the youngest and the oldest woman to have triumphed at the Games.

Fischer had actually retired, for a second time, in 2000 but was tempted back into a cameo for a film project in 2003. "Suddenly the curiosity was there again and I asked myself, 'What can I still achieve?'"

The mother-of-two from Brandenburg began training again and soon found she had the strength of old, as was demonstrated by her performances at these Games, when she more than held her own alongside younger team-mates. The German quartet were trailing in the K4 final but gradually overhauled the world champions, Hungary, to win by 0.19s.

In total, the remarkably versatile Fischer had now won eight Olympic gold medals and three silvers across 24 years, switching between K1, K2 and K4, kayaking in boats either solo, in a pair or a four, over distances from 200 metres to 1,000 metres.

By John Goodbody

Birgit Fischer (front) and her Germany team-mates (right to left) Maike Nollen, Katrin Wagner and Carolin Leonhardt during the K4 500 metres kayak event, which they went on to win at Athens 2004.

Super Swede on target in ninth Games

Men's free rifle 3x40 SH1 | Shooting

London Paralympics, 2012

These Paralympics were notable for many memorable performances but few can match what the Swedish shooter Jonas Jacobsson achieved. Competing in his ninth Paralympics, beginning with Moscow in 1980, he won yet another gold medal to bring his total to 17. This time, he was victorious in the men's free rifle three positions, one of his specialities.

Growing up with a disability in his lower limbs, he had to use a wheelchair since the age of seven, allowing him to take part in a variety of events but still concentrating on shooting. As he has said: "To be good at something strengthens self-confidence but it is important to have a humble attitude at the same time."

Jacobsson became so proficient that he was able to compete against non-disabled rivals. After securing four gold medals at the 2004 Paralympics, where he was victorious in both rifle and air rifle disciplines, he was a contender the following year in the Swedish Cup, open to both disabled and non-disabled competitors. On one day, he scored more highly than Matt Emmons, the 2004 Olympic champion in the 50-metre prone rifle event.

After further successes in 2008, he was the first Paralympian to be given the Svenska Gold medal, the most prestigious sporting award of his country.

By John Goodbody

Sweden's Jonas Jacobsson prepares his rifle during the shooting competition at the 2008 Paralympics, where he won three golds. His success in 2012 took him to 17 gold medals across his career.

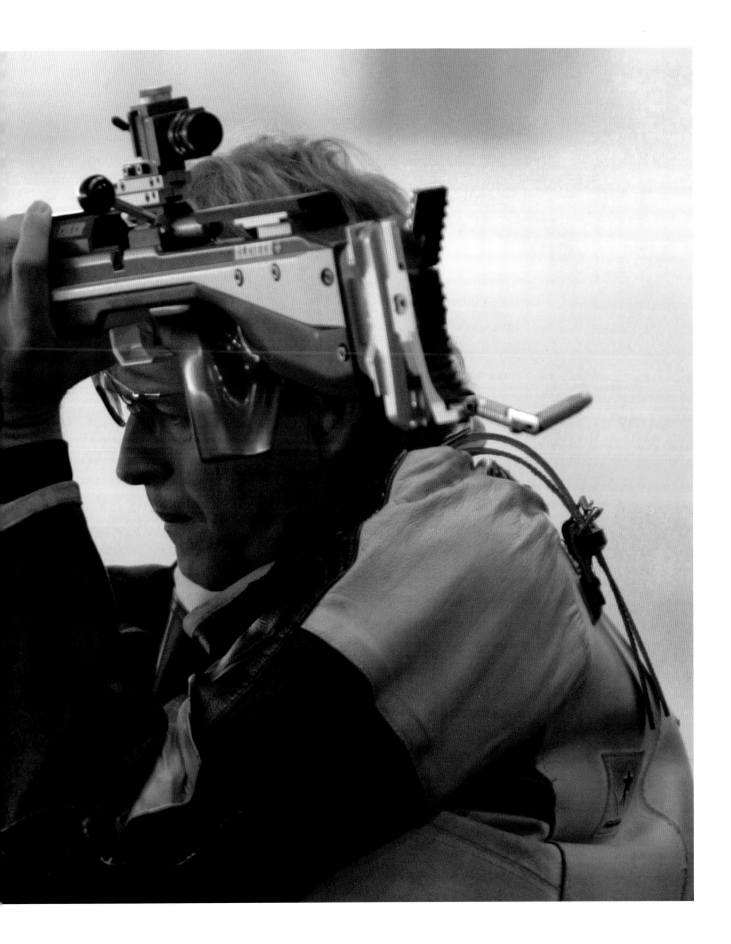

Petitclerc reigns supreme with fifth triumph

Women's T54 1,500 metres wheelchair | Athletics

Beijing Paralympics, 2008

The domination of Canadian Chantal Petitclerc over T54 wheelchair racing on the track was complete. She won the 1,500 metres title to add to the four shorter ones she had gained earlier in these Paralympics. Her fellow athletes regarded her with such respect and admiration, not just as a competitor, but also for the way she handled herself and spoke so eloquently about her fellow disabled competitors, notably through her work as an ambassador for the international organisation The Right to Play.

Petitclerc had carried the flag for disabled competitors ever since she herself suffered a life-changing accident at the age of 13, when a heavy barn door of the farm belonging to parents of a friend fell on her back, breaking lower vertebrae and so confining her to a wheelchair for the rest of her life. One actual flag she did carry was at the 2006 Commonwealth Games when she was given the honour at the opening ceremony of a competition that since 2002 has integrated both non-disabled and disabled athletes.

However, her gold medal in the 1,500 metres was not easily achieved. In a hectic finish she finished 2.11 seconds ahead of Britain's Shelly Woods in 3min 38.88s. Petitclerc had to use all her experience and speed shown in the shorter wheelchair races to clinch the title.

By John Goodbody

Canada's Chantal Petitclerc (left) edges past Liu Wenjun, of China, to win the T54 100 metres earlier in the Games..

Ennis rewards a nation's faith

Women's heptathlon | Athletics

London, 2012

By David Walsh, Olympic Stadium

There was something magical about how it all ended. The weight of a nation's expectation seemed no more than a feather as Jessica Ennis set off in the concluding 800 metres, determined that she would not only give the 80,000 spectators what they wanted but enjoy herself on the way. It wasn't a race. It was a celebration of British athleticism, one of the greatest we have seen.

Ennis had a 188-point lead over her closest rival, Austra Skujytė from Lithuania, at the start of the two-lap race but all that would happen was a lengthening of her advantage. The only danger to her gold medal was clipping the heels of a rival and falling. But she had thought of that because at the sound of the starter's gun, Ennis bolted to the front and established a five-yard lead.

As she moved round the track, each section of the crowd closest to her rose and showed their appreciation with thunderous support. She stayed out in front until 250m from the finish, when the German Lilli Schwarzkopf and the Russian, Tatyana Chernova, swept past her. That didn't threaten Ennis because Skujytė had been left well behind.

Ennis is as gritty as she is talented and after surrendering her lead to Schwarzkopf and Chernova, she bided her time in their slipstream, waiting until they had turned into the finishing straight before accelerating. And then she weaved her way off the inside and quickened past her rivals. The crowd went

Jessica Ennis celebrates winning gold at the end of the 800 metres, the final event of the heptathlon at London 2012.

wild, making as much noise as one has ever heard in an athletics stadium.

It seemed easy until you saw her fall on the track just beyond the finish line. Her eyes filled with tears but they were tears of joy, and the jubilant spectators never stopped showing their appreciation. For this was the victory that the nation most wanted and, not only had Ennis won, but she had done so in fantastic style.

The greatest challenge for Ennis was the expectation, the public's love for her, their almost desperate yearning that her career would have its greatest moment at her home Olympics. Partly because of her good looks but also because of her straightforward and easy-to-like personality, she became the poster athlete for the London Olympics.

The first achievement was to arrive in outstanding physical condition. Her wellbeing was shown in her very first event, the 100 metres hurdles when she ran an astonishing 12.54s. That gave her the perfect start but it wouldn't always be as smooth. In her very next discipline, the high jump, she failed twice at 1.83m and then twice again at 1.86m before clearing the bar.

Ennis would show the same grit in the shot put to find a throw that greatly limited the damage in one of her weaker events. But then in the 200 metres at the end of the first day, there was a reminder of her enormous class as she ran a magnificent 22.83s to establish a 184-point overnight lead.

After an average first effort in the long jump yesterday, she delivered a highly respectable 6.40m on her second jump and improved that to 6.48m. Ennis recorded another personal best in the javelin and then relished her two laps of honour in that wonderful 800 metres.

Ennis competes in the long jump during her gold-medal winning heptathlon campaign.

Ainslie crowned the greatest sailor

Men's Finn | Sailing

London, 2012

From Patrick Kidd, Weymouth Harbour

Ben Ainslie yesterday won his fourth gold medal at successive Olympic Games in a sport he took up when he was eight. He says he is unlikely to compete in 2016.

Britain's greatest Olympic sailor stood up in his boat and raised two flaming flares as a chorus of Rule Britannia broke out among the 5,000 spectators in the Nothe Gardens and the many more standing on the beaches around Weymouth Harbour. Ben Ainslie rules the waves once again.

Having also won Olympic silver when a teenager in 1996, Ainslie is now the most successful sailing Olympian, eclipsing the four golds that Paul Elvstrøm of Denmark won between 1948 and 1960.

It was another Dane who stood in Ainslie's way yesterday. Jonas Høgh-Christensen began the Olympics by beating Ainslie in six races. But Ainslie dragged himself back into contention last week and, going into yesterday's medal race, needed to finish ahead of Christensen to win gold. However, as they sparred at the back of the fleet, with Ainslie snatching the Dane's wind, another plot emerged. If Pieter-Jan Postma, from the Netherlands, could finish second and Ainslie ninth, the gold would go to Postma. Ainslie was winning his battle with Høgh-Christensen, but was unable to control the other side of the equation. However, the Dutchman slipped down the field at the last mark and Ainslie crossed the line to celebrations.

It is said that Ainslie has a sixth sense for reading the weather. He instinctively knows where to find the best wind, always scanning the waves for the traces of shadow that guide him. "It's something I have always been pretty good at," he says. "We lived in an isolated area, so I didn't have many friends around to kick a football with. To get out in the boat was my sort of escape."

Iain Percy, who has raced against Ainslie since they were teenagers, called him "the most competitive man in the world". Ainslie has proved that point many times, not least at the 2004 Olympics in Athens when he recovered from 24th place to seal his second gold. A third followed in Beijing despite going down with mumps just before the regatta. There has been little time for a love life but one female has been present through the last three Games – Rita, his nine-year-old dinghy. Most sailors get a new boat every two years but Ainslie says that there is "something special" about Rita.

Britain's Ben Ainslie in action at Weymouth Harbour during his victorious sailing campaign at London 2012.

Sensational Hoy surges to sixth gold

Men's keirin | Track cycling

London, 2012

By Ashling O'Connor, Olympic Velodrome

Sir Chris Hoy cycled into a wall of sound last night as six thousand cheering spectators in London's Velodrome willed him to summon a final surge and edge past his German rival for a record sixth gold medal. In the end, Hoy, 36, was three quarters of a bike length in front of Maximilian Levy when he crossed the line in the men's keirin race, to succeed Sir Steve Redgrave as the Briton to have won the most Olympic gold medals. As he collected his title, his second of these Games, tears streamed down his face. To a soundtrack of David Bowie's Heroes, his father, David, waved a banner: "Chris Hoy, the Real McHoy."

Later Hoy spoke of his confidence in the future of British sport. "The Brits historically got used to being plucky losers, that's started to change. You now have a group of young athletes who have only seen success."

The revolution in British cycling – masterminded by David Brailsford, whose glorious year includes Bradley Wiggins's victory in the Tour de France – goes on. When the track team returned from Beijing with seven of ten possible gold medals, it was a feat that everyone said could not be repeated. The International Cycling Union even changed the rules for the London Games, limiting the entrants to one per nation. It was interpreted as an attempt to clip the wings of Britain, which dominated the podium. But the team has ended these Games with the same tally: seven out of ten.

Britain's Chris Hoy is triumphant after winning the keirin at London 2012, the sixth gold of his Olympic career.

Britain's continued success has confounded the opposition. The French in particular were baffled, after appearing to catch Britain up at the world championships in April. Grégory Baugé, the triple world sprint champion, was so perplexed he questioned Jason Kenny, who beat him to the Olympic title, at their press conference. He demanded to know how he had been beaten. Brailsford came up with the answer: the British team had "specially round wheels", he joked.

The truth is that the opposition may have been hustled. Brailsford said that there was no secret to their success, just a philosophy of excellence, a method focused on every minute detail – the "aggregation of marginal gains" – and the best coaching. They played the psychological game "to devastating effect", according to Peter Keen, UK Sport's consultant, who set up cycling's first high-performance centre in Manchester in 1994.

Little things made the difference – such as packing away the custom-made, carbon fibre all-in-one handlebars and stems from Beijing and using lesser-quality aluminium pieces in the intervening years. It sharpens the skills and rivals falsely gain the impression that they are getting better. "They didn't use the best kit until it mattered – they effectively handicapped themselves," Keen said. "To know you are holding back is huge psychologically."

Hoy holds back his emotions in the velodrome at London 2012.

Superb Simmonds rides the adrenalin rush

Women's SM6 200 metres | Swimming

London Paralympics, 2012

By Alyson Rudd, Olympics Aquatic Centre

A final-leg surge secures medley title for a Briton. Butterfly, backstroke, breaststroke, freestyle; it sounds like a rhyme children might sing while skipping in the playground. Not when Ellie Simmonds is involved though. The 17-year-old tore ruthlessly through her SM6 200 metres individual medley yesterday to take her second gold medal of the Games.

This was a quite different sort of gold. Perhaps the second of a leading championship is less of an emotional maelstrom, but Simmonds needed a different approach. In the 400 metres freestyle there was a big unknown in the shape of Victoria Arlen, who had burst on to Simmonds's scene recording times that more than hinted at gold-medal form. Simmonds said that it had been 50-50 in her mind whether she would beat the American and that explained her tears. This time around she knew the odds were better than that.

And thank goodness she did because, although we knew she would win, it did not prevent gulps of panicked air all round as she trailed through the butterfly, backstroke and, yes, even breaststroke legs. If you had been blissfully unaware of the way Simmonds tackles this event you would have assumed Simmonds was out of it. Way out of it. A silver maybe. At best. Instead, she smashed her own world record again.

It has to be scary, doesn't it, lagging behind for so much of the race? Not for Simmonds. "I control my

Ellie Simmonds shows off her gold medal from the S6 400 metres freestyle, one of five events she won at London 2012.

own race and I know my advantage is my front crawl," she said. "I just go for it."

"That's really awesome," she said when told that the Prime Minister was watching, but she did not seem particularly overawed. After she had destroyed her challengers, urged on by a roar even louder than the one that had greeted her victory two days earlier, David Cameron was forced to take off his jacket. Yes, it is warm in the Aquatics Centre but watching Simmonds makes the coolest customer hot and flustered. Indeed, the Prime Minister looked more awestruck of her than she was of him when he presented the medals.

Simmonds claimed not to know how tearful she might become on the podium, but it was patently obvious she would maintain her composure, smile at the faces among the spectators that she recognised – and there were plenty – and absorb the beauty of the moment.

There is a fury to her strokes; she does not glide through the water, she chops at it. It is a curious sight because, yes, she attacks the water but when swimming at her best there is nothing brutal about it. Those who see her every day will tell you Simmonds can end up in a battle with the pool and her style will induce the odd wince as she uses energy rather than technique to win it. But when she is peaking both physically and mentally, as she is, happily, here, she looks formidable.

Simmonds surges forwards during the butterfly leg of the SM6 200 metres individual medley.

Peerless Riner sweeps up another title

Men's +100kg | Judo

Rio de Janeiro, 2016

FROM JOHN GOODBODY

Teddy Riner, fighting in the long tradition of outstanding French heavyweights, retained his Olympic title after dominating the competition, although his victory in the final against Japan's Hisayoshi Harasawa was an abject affair, with neither competitor attacking persistently. The 31-year-old Riner was given the decision, having been given one fewer penalty points than his opponent.

Still Riner had never been troubled by any fighter during the day's combats as he emulated his compatriot David Douillet, Olympic champion in 1996 and 2000, with this second gold medal. The tradition of French winners in this category was originally set by Angelo Parisi with his triumph in 1980.

All his rivals here were wary of Riner, who is 2.04 metres tall and weighs 140kg and is hugely athletic. After all, he has not lost a bout in six years and is renowned for his use of harai goshi (a sweeping hip throw), in which he takes a firm grip behind his opponent's head with his right hand, pulls him forward with the left arm, then sweeps his opponent's right leg away and lands on top of him. This move has terrorised rivals and only age is likely to threaten his superiority in the immediate future.

France's Teddy Riner (right) grapples with Hisayoshi Harasawa, of Japan, during the judo heavyweight final at Rio 2016. Riner won his second consecutive Olympic title.

Phenomenal Peaty restores British pride

Men's 100 metres breaststroke | Swimming

Rio de Janeiro, 2016

From Craig Lord

Four years ago, Great Britain's swimmers failed to turn up to their own party – last night they were the toast of the nation after Adam Peaty struck gold in the 100 metres breaststroke in Rio.

Peaty, who had dominated the heats, raced home to become the first British man to win an Olympic swimming title in 28 years – and the first GB swimmer to claim a gold medal in the pool since Rebecca Adlington's freestyle double in Beijing eight years ago. In claiming gold, Peaty also broke Team GB's medal duck at these Olympics. It was all a far cry from London 2012, when the tears rolled and the inquests began after the country's swimmers collected only two bronzes, courtesy of Adlington, and a silver, thanks to Michael Jamieson in the 200 metres breaststroke.

Peaty was not selected for those Games and was instead preparing to "go out to get drunk in a field" when he realised that he could be an Olympian if only he put his mind to it. Under the guidance of Mel Marshall, his coach at City of Derby, Peaty, 22, has matured into one of the finest swimmers of all time and the fastest man ever in the 100 metres breaststroke.

Adrian Moorhouse, the last British man to win an Olympic gold in the pool, triumphed in the same event by the smallest margin possible at the 1988

Games in Seoul – a mere 0.01s – but Peaty had looked a class above his rivals from the moment he clocked a world record in his opening heat. He lowered it to 57.13s in the final.

Moorhouse, there to witness the moment as a commentator, said: "It's like a loop has been closed, like the start of a new era."

As an 11-year-old Peaty was being beaten by ten-year-old girls. Marshall fished him out and "bullied" him into breaststroke because she saw "the spark ... and the way he moved in the water. He has something".

As his talent developed, Marshall worked at getting Peaty so far ahead of his peers that come the Olympic Games the tension would not become a factor. When Peaty turned in the two-lap race on 26.69s in the heats on the way to the world record, jaws dropped. Before Peaty set a world record for the solo 50 metres race at 26.42s, the mark had stood at 26.62s to Olympic 100 metres champion Cameron Van der Burgh, of South Africa. Beyond them, no other man has ever covered one lap of breaststroke as fast as Peaty did in Rio on the way to more history.

The world record would take "many weeks to sink in", he said, while he would for ever be grateful "to my best mate, Mel. She has been my rock. We've been striving, pushing the boundaries. There's been a lot of pain and hard work".

Britain's Adam Peaty breaks the world record for the 100 metres breaststroke at the 2016 Games in Rio de Janeiro.

Wiggins completes his masterpiece

Men's time trial | Road cycling

London, 2012

By Owen Slot, Hampton Court

Standing in the sun yesterday, receiving a medal in front of Hampton Court Palace, was like the last splash of colour in a work of art. Bradley Wiggins's Olympic gold had the leafy streets of Surrey howling with pleasure, but it was just the finishing touch in what has been arguably the greatest year by any road cyclist in history.

Wiggins is piling up outstanding achievements: never before had a Tour de France winner gone on to win an Olympic gold in the same year, and he now has four; Sir Steve Redgrave had seemed the ultimate British Olympian with six Olympic medals, but Wiggins has seven.

Never before had a British sportsman led so many denizens of the home counties into standing on the side of the road with huge red sideburns painted on their faces. They came out yesterday to watch him in the Olympic time trial, a 44-kilometre race-against-the-clock on a loop from Hampton Court, down to Cobham in Surrey, up the Thames and back. Wiggins was the penultimate rider on the course and as he swept through the Surrey streets it became increasingly clear that he was the fastest.

Tony Martin, of Germany, was his closest rival but the cheers of Wiggins's followers as he returned to Hampton Court told the story. He finished ahead of Martin by 42 seconds. His unbeaten record in time

Bradley Wiggins races to gold in the men's time trial at London 2012, adding to his Tour de France triumph earlier that summer.

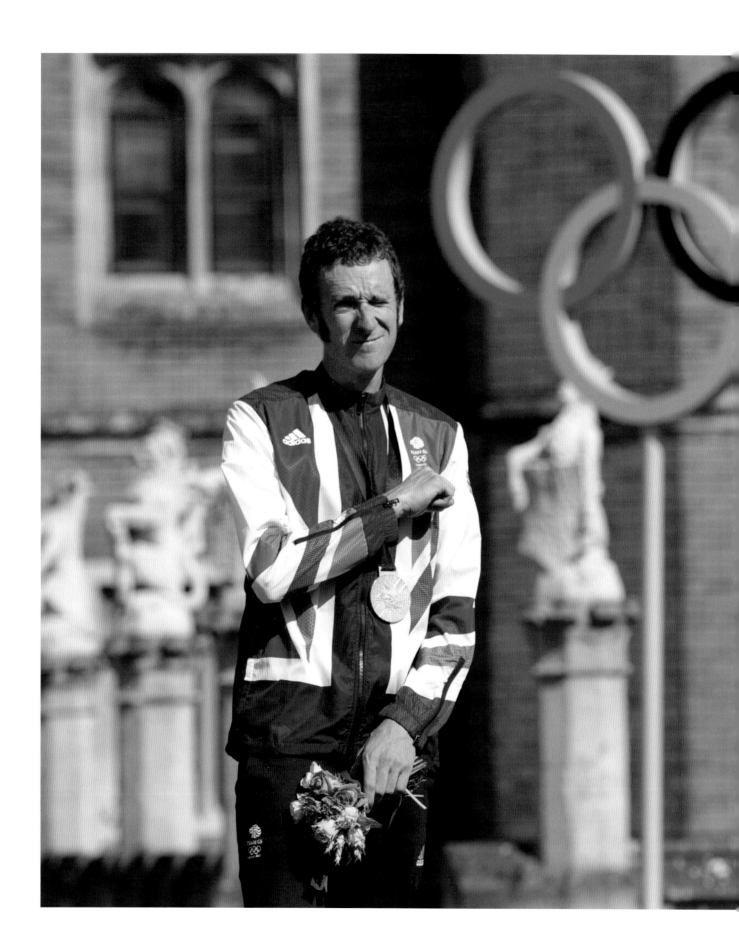

trials this year was intact. His newfound status as a man of the people is one he is beginning to grow into.

After his victory was assured and before receiving his medal, he got on his bicycle again and rode back up the road, in part to see his wife, but also, he explained, because of the elitism involved in getting into Olympic events.

"The great thing about cycling in Europe is anyone can come and watch it, whereas here [at the Olympics], you've got to be the chosen few to get in. It's a bit of a prawn sandwich-fest here. It's nice to go back out the gates there, to the public, and appreciate everything they did," he said.

It was "a shame" that the non-ticket-holding members of the public had not been allowed through the gates and up towards Hampton Court Palace to see the medal ceremony, he said.

Indeed, there was an irony about the grandeur of this setting. As Wiggins stood for his medal, he looked slightly embarrassed. He is not into pomp and grandeur. He said that it would be an honour if, as seems likely, a knighthood came his way, but he would not use the title. "Sir Wiggo" did not sound right, he said.

Wiggins salutes the British fans on the podium for the individual time trial.

Even rivals applaud Uchimura's feat

Men's individual all-around | Gymnastics

Rio de Janeiro, 2016

FROM JOHN GOODBODY

No gymnast in history, male or female, has achieved what Kohei Uchimura did today, completing a supremacy that not even any of the stars of the past have managed. He has won every annual global all-around title from the world championships in London in 2009 to his second Olympic gold medal yesterday, eight successive victories.

His compatriot Sawao Kato matched him in the Olympics, with two successive golds in 1968 and 1972, as did Pierre Payssé, Albert Braglia and Viktor Chukharin over the course of the twentieth century. However, none of them enjoyed the consistent run of successes of Uchimura, who has achieved such consistency over his demanding and adventurous routines, where gymnasts repeatedly try original moves to get a higher tariff rating. He did fall a few times in qualifying for the all-around final in 2012 but was unblemished here. His fellow athletes were applauding him. Well they might.

Over the course of his career, many gymnasts have opted to concentrate on one apparatus, while still achieving a high level on the remaining five. Uchimura has been different. In fact, his only Olympic medal on an individual apparatus was the silver he took on the floor exercises in 2012.

Instead, he has built up a uniform level of performance across the other five as well: namely the rings, high bar, parallel bars, vault and pommel horse and was rewarded again today. It brought him another gold medal to add to the team title he won with Japan three days ago. He was magnificent.

Above – Kohei Uchimura, of Japan, performs on the parallel bars ahead of winning all-around gold at the Rio Olympics.

Opposite – Uchimura, practises his vault routine ahead of winning all-around gold.

Whitlock scoops unexpected gold

Men's floor exercise and pommel horse | Gymnastics

Rio de Janeiro, 2016

From Alyson Rudd

Max Whitlock's name will come to be part of Olympic folklore. The 23-year-old catapulted Britain to a place among the elite of the gymnastics world in the space of one glorious evening after winning Olympic titles on both the pommel and the floor.

He had been on course to win here on the pommel horse since he took the world title in November but his victory in the floor event was astonishing, emotional and entirely unexpected. It meant that Britain's first ever Olympic gymnastics gold medal turned up when no one was really looking for it as the favourites for the floor title were rocked by the febrile atmosphere in a packed arena.

In the midst of what might be termed outrageous behaviour by the Brazilian crowd, Whitlock held his nerve to claim the Olympic floor exercise title ahead of Kenzo Shirai, of Japan, who was the man to beat having won the world title in November. Whitlock then managed to rein in the emotions of being a history maker to complete a near faultless routine on the pommel.

The floor final was a four-way battle between Britain, Japan, the United States and Brazil, the only nations to have qualified for the exercise, and it all began with Kohei Uchimura, the all-around champion here and arguably the greatest male gymnast of all time, stumbling off the mat boundary. His qualification score was 15.533, yesterday he was awarded 15.241.

Immediately the crowd sensed an upset could be on the cards and Brazil's Diego Hypólito brought the stadium to life with a vibrant piece of accuracy. They love their gymnastics here and it must have been hard for the judges to block out the adoration. If exercises were scored by screech level alone then Brazil would have mopped up most of the gymnastics medals in Rio.

Hypólito scored 15.533, which was met with approval in the stands as it put him ahead of the great Uchimura. His lead did not last long, however, because Whitlock was excellent, finishing with a crisp triple twist to score 15.633. Whitlock got lucky, he competed while the locals were still basking in Hypólito's excellence.

Thereafter it got nasty. As far as the vast majority watching were concerned, it was all about keeping Brazil in with a chance of a medal and the atmosphere played havoc with all who followed Whitlock. The Briton watched them, wrapped in the union flag, with a grin emerging on his face as it became clear that the gold was his.

Britain's Max Whitlock performs his winning routine on the pommel horse at Rio 2016. The Briton won three golds at the Games.

Brownlee brothers go flat out for historic double

Men's triathlon

Rio de Janeiro, 2016

By Fariha Karim

The Brownlee brothers swam, cycled and ran their way into Olympic history yesterday after becoming Britain's first siblings to take gold and silver in the same event. Alistair Brownlee, the elder of the Yorkshire-born brothers by two years, became the first Olympic triathlon champion to retain his title after winning in a time of 1hr 45min 1s. Jonny followed six seconds behind.

The 28-year-old gold medallist slowed to a saunter as he reached the blue carpet at the finish after a 1.5km swim, 40km bike ride and 10km run, crossing the line with a Union Jack in one hand and Yorkshire rose flag in the other. The men – only the ninth pair of brothers in summer and winter Games to finish with a gold and silver in the same event, and the first since 1960 – described how they had spent the past year of training "killing each other" every day in their quest to share the podium in Rio.

"Every day this year has been so hard," an emotional Alistair, 28, said after the race. "I've woken up in pain every day. God, that was so hard. I don't know about Jonny, but he's killed me in training every day." He said, however, that he had been "pretty confident we were going to take the first and second", though conceded that he "didn't know entirely which way".

Jonny, who won bronze in London, added: "I'm incredibly proud. I'm used to getting beaten by Alistair at the Olympics and that was the dream result. To get gold and silver I'm incredibly proud. I like to think I'm a tough Yorkshireman, but I was emotional at the end."

This time last year Jonny had a stress fracture in his left leg and Alistair's Olympic ambitions were on hold with an ankle injury. Celebrating the Brownlee brothers' success was their uncle, Simon Hearnshaw, 54, a triathlete who first encouraged the brothers to get into the sport. He described how the brothers had practised for Brazil by cycling inside saunas. "It's warm out there – it's not great for a couple of Yorkshire lads," he said.

They were joined in Rio by their father, Keith Brownlee, a former paediatrician who now works for the Cystic Fibrosis Trust, and their mother, Cathy Hearnshaw, a GP. Ed Brownlee, 20, their youngest son, stayed in England. He previously told his brothers that "triathlon is a rubbish sport for soft people" but said last night that he may have to go back on his words.

Opposite Top – *Britain's Alistair and Jonathan Brownlee enter the changeover zone neck and neck during the men's triathlon at Rio 2016.*

Opposite Bottom – *Alistair Brownlee (right) and his brother Jonathan collapse in exhaustion after winning triathlon gold and silver respectively.*

Sifan Hassan, of the Netherlands,
is overcome with emotion on
winning the 10,000 metres at
Tokyo 2020.

Hassan joins legends with glorious hat-trick

Women's 10,000 metres | Athletics

Tokyo, 2020

Sifan Hassan achieved a unique Olympic treble here, victorious in the 10,000 metres after her triumphs in the 1,500 and 5,000 metres. No male or female has matched this feat in the history of the Games and it required a range of running ability, which she demonstrated in a race of enthralling interest.

For lap after lap, Hassan, representing the Netherlands but of Ethiopian origin, had her stamina stretched by the pace-setting of Letesenbet Gidey of Ethiopia but with 200 metres left, Hassan, 28, moved up a gear, rounded Gidey and sprinted for home. Chased despairingly by the silver medallist Kalkidan Gezahegne of Bahrain, another athlete born in Ethiopia, and the third-placed Gidey, Hassan finished clear by 0.46 seconds in 29 minutes 55.32 seconds.

Speaking of her triple, she said afterwards: "We women are very capable. We are a lot stronger." The only comparison in the panoply of Olympic athletics is with two legends. First is with Paavo Nurmi, greatest of all 'The Flying Finns', who in 1924 won five gold medals, including the 1,500 metres and 5,000 metres in Paris as well as the cross country and two team races. He probably would have won the 10,000 metres but the Finnish authorities prevented him from entering. The other comparison is with Emil Zátopek, who, in 1952, took gold medals in the 5,000 metres, 10,000 metres and the marathon, never achieved before or since.

By John Goodbody

Storey storms to record 17th title

Women's para C4-5 road race | Cycling

Tokyo Paralympics, 2020

By Emma Yeomans

Sixteen years after an ear infection forced her to quit swimming, Dame Sarah Storey has cycled into the record books with a 17th Paralympic gold medal. The 43-year-old is now Britain's most successful ever Paralympian.

She won her first gold aged 14 at the 1992 Barcelona Games, as a swimmer. After competing in the pool at three further Games she switched to cycling in 2005 after ear infections left her with chronic fatigue syndrome.

She won her first cycling gold in 2008 in Beijing, and arrived in Tokyo with 50 world championship or Paralympic medals in the sport. But her greatest achievement is returning to sport after becoming a mother, she said.

Storey, who was born without a functioning left hand after her arm was tangled in the umbilical cord in the womb, said: "Being able to come back after two pregnancies – that's got to be my biggest achievement.

"I never expected to come back [from having children], and it was certainly not a pressure that I had to come back."

She started swimming aged ten but was told she had begun too late to be good at it. She said she was a "walking conversation stopper" as a child, arriving at school with wet hair from the pool, and was frequently bullied.

Forced out of the pool by ear infections, she took up cycling to maintain fitness, and within a year had broken a paracycling world record.

Sarah Storey, of Great Britain, on track during the women's C5 3,000 metre individual pursuit, the first of three events in which she won gold at the 2020 Paralympics.

Britain acclaim golden couple

Men's and women's track cycling

Tokyo, 2020

From Matt Dickinson, Chief Sports Writer

Jason Kenny became the most successful British Olympian in history by winning a seventh gold, out of a total of nine medals, but the track cyclist happily expects his wife, Laura, to receive more attention than him.

The couple now rank as the most successful male and female British Olympians, with 15 medals, 12 of them gold. They are also the Games' most decorated married couple.

But she will still attract more sponsorship deals. "Probably because she is generally nicer than I am," he said. "Also, she is infinitely better looking. It's fine, it's the way it is, she is a very inspiring character. She is lovely, obviously – that's why I married her – but I am a bit boring."

There was nothing dull about the way that Kenny won in Shizuoka to overtake Sir Bradley Wiggins (eight medals, five gold) and Sir Chris Hoy (seven medals, six gold).

Kenny won his seventh gold in the men's keirin. He caught his rivals napping by charging into an unassailable lead with three laps to go. Last week, Laura won her fifth gold, in the Madison, to go with a silver in the pursuit.

Jason said that the couple were looking forward to returning home to be with their son Albie, three. "We have not seen him for two weeks," he said. "It has been really tough. It will be nice to get back and be daft again, give him a hug."

Jason and Laura Kenny pose with their medals at Tokyo 2020, where they became the most successful male and female British Olympians.

Index

Acknowledgements

There are many people who deserve our thanks for helping to arrange this project, and for providing valuable technical and artistic support. In particular, the News UK archive team helped us source the most captivating journalism and images. At HarperCollins, Harley Griffiths and Samuel Fitzgerald have provided guidance throughout the process, and Kevin Robbins lent his design expertise to the cover. Thanks to Sir Steve Redgrave for supplying the foreword, and to Melanie Clift for her help in arranging that. Finally, our thanks go to all of the Times writers over the years, without whom this book would not have been possible.

Photo Credits

Jacket (front) Ian Waldie/Getty Images;
Jacket (back) HABANS Patrice/Getty Images;
Hard cover (front) Gareth Copley/PA/Alamy Stock Photo;
Hard cover (back) B.J. Warnick/Newscom/Alamy Stock Photo;
P4-5 The Asahi Shimbun/Getty Images;
P7 Andrew Cowie/Shutterstock;
P10-11 Cameron Spencer/Getty Images;
P12-13 AP/Alamy Stock Photo;
P14 (top) The Times/News Licensing; (bottom) Süddeutsche Zeitung/Alamy Stock Photo;
P16-17 Kemsley/The Times/News Licensing;
P19 (top) PA/Alamy Stock Photo; (bottom) Alamy Stock Photo;
P20-21 Bettmann/Getty Images;
P22-23 Zuma/Alamy Stock Photo;
P24-25 Keystone Press/Alamy Stock Photo;
P27 Bettmann/Getty Images;
P28-29 Katsumi Kasahara/AP/Alamy Stock Photo;
P31 Lynne Sladky/AP/Alamy Stock Photo;
P32-33 Back Page Images/Shutterstock;
P34-35 Marc Aspland/The Times/News Licensing;
P36-37 Gareth Copley/PA/Alamy Stock Photo;
P38 Zuri Swimmer/Alamy Stock Photo;
P39 Niday Picture Library/Alamy Stock Photo;
P40-41 Marc Aspland/The Times/News Licensing;
P43 Richard Pelham/The Times/News Licensing;
P45 Marc Aspland/The Times/News Licensing;
P46-47 Marc Aspland/The Times/News Licensing;
P48-49 Marc Aspland/The Times/News Licensing;
P50-51 Corbis Historical/Getty Images;
P52-53 The Asahi Shimbun/Getty Images;
P54-55 PA/Alamy Stock Photo;

P57 (top)Ian Stewart/The Times/News Licensing; (bottom) The Times/News Licensing;
P58-59 AP/Alamy Stock Photo;
P60-61 Richard Pelham/The Times/News Licensing;
P62-63 ANL/Shutterstock;
P65 Marc Aspland/Tmes Newspapers;
P66-67 AP/Alamy Stock Photo;
P68-69 PA/Alamy Stock Photo;
P70-71 Empics/Alamy Stock Photo;
P73 (top) S&G/Alamy Stock Photo; (bottom) S&G/Alamy Stock Photo;
P74-75 AP/Alamy Stock Photo;
P76-77 H. Olle Seijbold/The Times/News Licensing;
P78-79 Chris Smith/The Times/News Licensing;
P80-81 Getty Images;
P82 Mirrorpix/Alamy Stock Photo;
P83 Leifer/Getty Images;
P84 Süddeutsche Zeitung/Alamy Stock Photo;
P85 The Asahi Shimbun/Getty Images;
P86 Deither Endlicher/AP/Alamy Stock Photo;
P87 Rusty Kennedy/AP/Alamy Stock Photo;
P88-89 HABANS Patrice/Getty Images;
P90 Empics/Alamy Stock Photo;
P93 AP/Alamy Stock Photo;
P94 AP/Alamy Stock Photo;
P95 Bettmann/Getty Images;
P97 Derek Cattani/Shutterstock;
P99 AP/Alamy Stock Photo;
P100 (top) Herbert Knosowski/AP/Alamy Stock Photo; (bottom) Ira Gostin/AP/Alamy Stock Photo;
P102-103 S&G/Alamy Stock Photo;
P104-105 Ron Kuntz/AP/Alamy Stock Photo;

P106 Marc Aspland/The Times/News Licensing;
P109 (top) Milst Bicanski/Stringer/Getty Images; (bottom) Paul Rogers/The Times/News Licensing;
P110-111 Max Scheler/Süddeutsche Zeitung/Alamy Stock Photo;
P112-113 Everett Collection/Alamy Stock Photo;
P114-115 Neal Simpson/PA/Alamy Stock Photo;
P116 AP/Alamy Stock Photo;
P119 Douglas Miller/Getty Images;
P120-121 Süddeutsche Zeitung/Alamy Stock Photo;
P122 Allstar/Alamy Stock Photo;
P125 (top) Marc Aspland/The Times/News Licensing; (bottom) PA/Alamy Stock Photo;
P126 Jonathan Short/AP/Alamy Stock Photo;
P127 The Times/News Licensing;
P128-129 PCN/Alamy Stock Photo;
P130-131 AP/Alamy Stock Photo;
P132-133 Chronicle/Alamy Stock Photo;
P134-135 AP/Alamy Stock Photo;
P136 PA/Alamy Stock Photo;
P139 PA/Alamy Stock Photo;
P140 PA/Alamy Stock Photo;
P141 AP/Alamy Stock Photo;
P143 Chronicle/Alamy Stock Photo;
P144-145 Split Seconds/Alamy Stock Photo;
P146 The History Collection/Alamy Stock Photo;
P148-149 Granger/Alamy Stock Photo;
P150-151 Mark Kauffman/The LIFE Picture Collection/Shutterstock;
P153 Bettmann/Getty Images;
P154 (top) Alfred Harris/The Times/News Licensing; (bottom) Alfred Harris/The Times/News Licensing;

P156-157 Stringer/Getty Images;
P159 AP/Alamy Stock Photo;
P160 Getty Images;
P162 AP/Alamy Stock Photo;
P163 AP/Alamy Stock Photo;
P164-165 AP/Alamy Stock Photo;
P166 Keystone/Zuma/Shutterstock;
P167 NCAA Photos/Getty Images;
P168 Denis Paquin/AP/Alamy Stock Photo;
P170 Sports Illustrated/Getty Images;
P171 PCN/Alamy Stock Photo;
P172 Doug Mills/AP/Alamy Stock Photo;
P174-175 Andy Hooper/Daily Mail/Shutterstock;
P176-177 David Ashdown/Alamy Stock Photo;
P178-179 Graham Hughes/The Times/News Licensing;
P181 Pictorial Press/Alamy Stock Photo;
P182 AP/Alamy Stock Photo;
P184-185 The Asahi Shimbun/Getty Images;
P186-187 The Asahi Shimbun/Getty Images;
P188 S&G/Alamy Stock Photo;
P190-191 DPA/Alamy Stock Photo;
P192 Mirrorpix/Alamy Stock Photo;

P193 Interfoto/Alamy Stock Photo;
P194-195 Ole Frederiksen/AP/Alamy Stock Photo;
P196 Hulton Archive/Getty Images;
P198-199 Pepe Franco/Getty Images;
P200-201 Doug Mills/AP/Alamy Stock Photo;
P202-203 Allstar/Alamy Stock Photo;
P204-205 Neal Simpson/PA/Alamy Stock Photo;
P206 PA/Alamy Stock Photo;
P208 B.J. Warnick/Alamy Stock Photo;
P210-211 DPA/Alamy Stock Photo;
P212-213 Armando Franca/AP/Alamy Stock Photo;
P214-215 Elizabeth Dalziel/AP/Alamy Stock Photo;
P216-217 Ng Han Guan/AP/Alamy Stock Photo;
P218-219 Marc Aspland/The Times/News Licensing;
P220-221 Richard Pelham/The Times/News Licensing;
P222 Dorset Media Service/Alamy Stock Photo;
P224-225 Marc Aspland/The Times/News Licensing;

P226-227 Marc Aspland/The Times/News Licensing;
P228-229 Graham Hughes/The Times/News Licensing;
P230-231 Graham Hughes/The Times/News Licensing;
P232-233 B.J. Warnick/Newscom/Alamy Stock Photo;
P235 PCN/Alamy Stock Photo;
P236-237 Graham Hughes/The Times/News Licensing;
P238-239 Graham Hughes/The Times/News Licensing;
P240 Lukas Schulze/DPA/Alamy Stock Photo;
P241 Paul Kitzagi Jr/Zuma/Alamy Stock Photo;
P243 Marc Aspland/The Times/News Licensing;
P245 (top) Foto Arena LTDA/Alamy Stock Photo; (bottom) Richard Pelham/The Times/News Licensing;
P246-247 NTB/Alamy Stock Photo;
P248-249 Aflo Co./Alamy Stock Photo;
P250-251 ANL/Shutterstock;
P256 Hulton Archive/Getty Images

Photo captions

Jacket (front)
Kelly Holmes waves to the crowd after winning gold in the women's 1,500 metres at Athens 2004. The feat marked the pinnacle of an athletics career hitherto hampered by injury and cemented her place in British Olympic history.

Jacket (back) and page 86-87
Tommie Smith (centre) and John Carlos (right) perform the Black Power salute during the medal ceremony for the 200 metres at the 1968 Olympics in Mexico City. Australian Peter Norman (left) wears a human rights badge in solidarity.

Hard cover (front)
Tanni Grey-Thompson celebrates her 100 metres victory in the T53 wheelchair event at Athens 2004, the Briton's eleventh Paralympic gold.

Hard cover (back)
Sweden's Armand Duplantis celebrates clearing the bar in front of an empty grandstand in the mens' pole vualt final at Tokyo 2020.

Page 4-5
Captain Masae Kasai receives her gold medal after leading the Japanese women's volleyball team to victory at Tokyo 1964.

Page 10-11
Usain Bolt grins at the camera before crossing the line in the 100 metres semi-final at Rio 2016.

Page 48-49
Britain's women celebrate winning hockey gold at Rio 2016 after a late equaliser took the final to a penalty shootout.

Page 66-67
Michael Phelps faces off against Milorad Cavic before the final of the men's 100 metres butterfly at Beijing 2008.

Page 114-115
British track cyclist Chris Boardman during the individual pursuit at Barcelona 1992, where he won gold on his revolutionary Lotus bike.

Page 128-129
Kerri Strug is carried onto the podium by her coach Béla Károlyi after her performance with an injured ankle secured gymnastics gold for the United States at the 1996 Games.

Page 178-179
Ellie Simmonds on her way to winning the women's S6 400 metres freestyle at London 2012.

Page 256
Sebastian Coe and Steve Ovett embrace after the 800 metres final at the 1984 Olympics in Los Angeles.

Writers featured

Neil Allen, Simon Barnes, Pat Butcher, Peter Bryan, Matt Dickinson, Robert Dineen, Steven Downes, Norman Fox, Sydney Friskin, John Goodbody, Julia Gregory, James Hider, Oliver Holt, Rob Hughes, Fariha Karim, Patrick Kidd, Ron Lewis, John Livesey, Andrew Longmore, Craig Lord, Ashling O'Connor, David Powell, Matthew Pryor, Jim Railton, Alyson Rudd, Owen Slot, Nicholas Soames, Cliff Temple, David Walsh, David Watts, Emma Yeomans